SINGING PSALMS

*Responsorial Psalms
set to Simple Chant
Year A*

Music by
Alison Cadden
Peter Thompson

THE COLUMBA PRESS

Published by
The Columba Press
55A Spruce Avenue,
Stillorgan Industrial Park,
Blackrock
Co Dublin

Music engraving and typesetting by
Michael Walsh at MusicPrint, Chichester

Printed in Ireland by ColourBooks, Dublin

ISBN 9781 85607 722 4

Contents

FOREWORD

The worship of Almighty God engages heart and mind and spirit. It has been a human aspiration and human activity for as long as homo sapiens, and indeed more primitive forms of humanity, have inhabited the earth. The psalms and especially the singing of the psalms have been at the heart of the Judaeo-Christian approach to worship for fully three thousand years. The psalms connect us to the Jerusalem Temple, the synagogue, the liturgy of the first Christians, the monastic tradition, and the traditions and forms of cathedral and parish worship throughout the ages. There is a universality about the psalms which unites Christians of every tradition. When we lift our voices and thus our eyes and hearts to sing the psalms we articulate our unity as a people before the throne of grace.

The psalms explore the whole spectrum from the darkest moments of human frailty and despair on the one hand and the most radiant experiences of heavenly rapture on the other. They take us within ourselves, around ourselves and above ourselves in what is an almost complete articulation of the human condition and our complex relationship with God.

These are reasons why we must guard with our lives the inheritance we have in the psalms and ensure that they never become deleted from our books of worship. Therefore I joyfully acclaim the completion of Alison Cadden and Peter Thompson's work in seeking to provide easily accessible, melodic and rhythmical settings which enable the psalms to be fully incorporated in contemporary worship even where musical resources are severely limited. The singing of the psalms has changed and evolved over the three or more millennia we have known them. This work will take its place in that distinguished and, most importantly, living and lively tradition.

+Alan Armagh:

October 2010

INTRODUCTION
Singing Psalms, Year A

This publication of Singing Psalms – Year A completes the lectionary cycle, albeit in a roundabout format! It hardly seems possible that three years have passed since we piloted a sample selection of Psalms for Year A at Eastertide which were generally well received, and are now able to offer this third and final volume for use throughout the Church of Ireland and further afield.

To complete the lectionary provision, this volume includes Psalms for Saints Days and Holy Days, detailed as Appendix 1, and Psalms for the Easter Vigil, listed as Appendix 2. To allow space for these additions, we have cross-referenced certain days (Christmas – Epiphany 1, Candlemas, Ash Wednesday, Mothering Sunday, Holy Week & Easter Day) to the other volumes in the series where there are already two alternative settings for each of these days. Many psalms occur in each of the three years, and in some cases a third alternative setting is provided in this volume. To allow settings of any particular psalm to be located with ease, a master index is provided in this volume which cross-references all three volumes by psalm number.

During the past two years since the production of the first volume in this series we have been indebted to, and encouraged by, the many people – musicians, clergy and members of congregations – who have offered positive comments and constructive criticism, We are thankful to all who have taken the time and trouble to communicate their opinions which have helped us to refine this volume and give it its present shape. We have enjoyed our contacts with friends old and new and look forward to meeting many of you as we launch this final volume and present workshops across the country.

It has been both a joy and privilege to set these holy texts to music. We hope the settings will encourage participation in psalm singing in parishes the length and breadth of Ireland. We offer them wiith heartfelt thanks to God for the gift of music, and we trust that our efforts will serve as a fragrant offering to his praise and glory.

Alison Cadden & Peter Thompson

St Michael & All Angels, 29 September 2010

PERFORMANCE NOTES

Responsorial Psalmody allows for flexibility in approach which can be tailored to the circumstances and resources of the local church.

The format is as follows:
• The Response is introduced on organ or piano.
• The Choir/Cantor sings the Response.
• The Congregation repeats the Response.
• The Choir/Cantor chants the first set of verses.
• The Congregation replies with the Response.
• This pattern continues, the psalm ending with the Response.

Each psalm setting may be identified by the composer's initials in the top right-hand corner. There is some stylistic variation in detail and approach.

The psalm settings designated AJC are by Alison Cadden. The Response is sung in Unison, and the chant for the verses may be sung either in Unison or in four-part harmony (SATB). In the chant, the first chord is intoned until the end of the line when the chord changes, indicated by the underlined word or phrase; this pattern continues to the end of the group of verses (usually 2), so that there are 2 chords x 4 lines (cf. Advent I: Psalm 25).

When the chant ends with a suspension/resolution in either Alto or Tenor (or occasionally both, eg. Psalms 42 & 43, Proper 7 Continuous), this may be taken as two minims, provided the Response begins on the first beat (or downbeat) of the bar. If the Response begins on the last beat (or upbeat), the suspension may be taken as a minim and the resolution as a crotchet, to allow for seamless flow between chant and Response (eg Song of Isaiah, Advent 3). Occasionally the Response is in compound time; when this happens the format for the suspension/resolution is two dotted crotchets (eg. Psalm 118, Palm Sunday), or a dotted crotchet followed by a crotchet (eg. Psalm 29, Epiphany 1).

The psalms designated PT are by Peter Thompson. Both response and chant are intended for unison singing throughout. The chants are a form of simplified Anglican chant, and should feel 'familiar' to those used to traditional chanting. There are only 9 chants used in the three-year cycle, which, with regular use will become familiar not just to the choir, but also to the congregation. Each chant consists of 4 sections or quarters – essentially each is a reciting note with a simple inflection. Pointing marks in the verses have been kept to a minimum. The *barline* signifies the change from reciting note to inflection. In each *inflection*, normally only one syllable is sung to each note (except the last, which often may have multiple syllables). *Underlining* indicates where more than one syllable should be sung to the same note and occasionally one syllable is to be sung to two notes. This is indicated by the presence of an umlaut, e.g. page 1, verse 6, "löve".

In both Alison's and Peter's settings, an asterisk in the middle of a line indicates a break, and a break should also be taken between each line. In some psalms, for reasons of space, two lines of the psalm are printed as a single line of text. In these instances, an asterisk indicates a break between the lines. A break need not be taken at each comma, a slight lengthening of the syllable should usually be sufficient. At a semi-colon a break may be taken, if appropriate. The key issue is to make sense of the words – to let them dominate the music, and not the reverse. A well chanted psalm should sound very similar to a well read psalm.

It may be possible to shorten some of the lengthier psalms, where necessary. This should always be done sensitively and in the context of the wider ministry of the word.

ACKNOWLEDGMENTS

Yet again we are deeply grateful to Dr Michael Walsh for making sense of, and expertly editing, our scribblings on Sibelius. His commitment to this project from earliest days, and his utter professionalism at all times, have impressed us greatly. It has been a pleasure to work with him on this project from start to finish, even if largely electronically!

We wish to thank the Most Reverend Alan Harper, Archbishop of Armagh, for taking time to write the Foreword to this final volume.

Thanks are due once again to Brenda Thompson for editorial assistance, and to Paul Harron, Church of Ireland Press Officer, for help with publicity.

We have greatly valued the ongoing support of our colleagues on the Liturgical Advisory Committee. Their enthusiasm and encouragement have kept us going during marathon moments!

We greatly appreciate those within the Church of Ireland who have responded with their experiences of using the material, and for their constructive criticism.

Finally, our sincerest thanks belong to our long-suffering families!

Alison would like to dedicate this final volume to the older generations within her family: her husband Terence, her father Jim and stepmother Elizabeth, and in thankful remembrance of her late mother Ellen and grandmother Sadie, both of whom nurtured her early love of music.

Peter would like to dedicate this final volume to his parents Alrick and Valerie, and in thankful remembrance of his late grandmother Sally who encouraged him so greatly to develop his musical gifts.

Thanks be to God!

Advent 1

Ps 122

R v.1

PT

I was glad when they said to me, 'Let us go to the house of the Lord.'

2   And now our feet | are standing
     within your gates | O Jerusalem;
3   Jerusalem built | as a city
     that is at unity | in itself.

4   Thither the tribes go up * the tribes of | the Lord,
     as is decreed for Israel * to give thanks to the name | of the Lord.
5   For there are set the | thrones of judgement,
     the thrones of the | house of David.

6   O pray for the peace of | Jerusalem:
     'May they prosper who | löve you.
7   'Peace be with|in your walls
     and tranquillity with|in your palaces.'

8   For my kindred and compan|ions' sake,
     I will pray that | peace be with you.
9   For the sake of the house of the | Lord our God,
     I will seek to | do you good.

Advent 2

Ps 72 v.1-7, 18-19
R v.18

AJC

Blessed be the Lord, the God of Israel, who alone does wonderful things.

1   Give the king your judgements, O God,
      and your righteousness to the son of a king.
2   Then shall he judge your people righteously
      and your poor with justice.

3   May the mountains bring forth peace,
      and the little hills righteousness for the people.
4   May he defend the poor among the people,
      deliver the children of the needy and crush the oppressor.

5   May he live as long as the sun and moon endure,
      from one generation to another.
6   May he come down like rain upon the mown grass,
      like the showers that water the earth.

7   In his time shall righteousness flourish,
      and abundance of peace till the moon shall be no more.
19   And blessed be his glorious name for ever.
      May all the earth be filled with his glory. Amen. Amen.

Advent 3

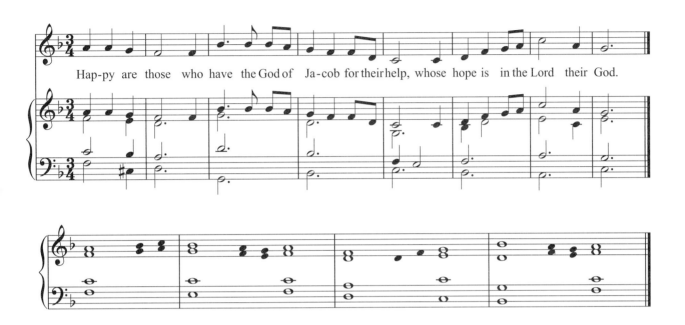

Hap-py are those who have the God of Ja-cob for their help, whose hope is in the Lord their God.

Happy are those who have the God of Jacob for their help, whose hope is in the Lord their God;

5   Who made heaven and earth, the sea and all that | is in them;
         who keeps his | promise for ever;

6   Who gives justice to those that | suffer wrong
         and bread to | those who hunger.

7   The Lord looses those that | are bound;
         the Lord opens the eyes | of the blind;

8   The Lord lifts up those who | are bowed down;
         the Lord | loves the righteous;

9   The Lord watches over the stranger in | the land;
         he upholds the orphan and widow; but the way of the wicked he turns | upside down.

10   The Lord shall reign for ever, your | God, O Zion,
         throughout all generations. | Alleluia.

Advent 3
Alternative Canticle

Magnificat

R v.3

The Almighty has done great things for me, and holy is his name.

1   My soul proclaims the greatness of | the Lord:
    my spirit rejoices in | God my Saviour.

2   Who has looked with favour on his | lowly servant:
    from this day all generations will | call me blessed

4   God has mercy on those | who fear him:
    from generation to | generation.

5   The Lord has shown strength | with his arm:
    and scattered the proud in | their conceit.

6   Casting down the mighty from | their thrones:
    and lifting | up the lowly.

7   God has filled the hungry | with good things:
    and sent the | rich a-way empty.

8   He has come to the aid of his ser|vant Israel:
    to remember the | promise of mercy,

9   The promise made | to our forebears:
    to Abraham and his | children for ever.

Advent 4

Ps 80 v1-8, 18-20

R v.8

AJC

Turn us a-gain, O God of hosts; show the light of your count-en-ance, and we shall be saved.

Turn us again, O God of hosts;
show the light of your countenance, and we shall be saved.

1   Hear, O Shepherd of <u>Israel</u>,
     you that led Joseph like a <u>flock</u>;
2   Shine forth, you that are enthroned upon the <u>cherubim</u>,
     before Ephraim, Benjamin and Man<u>asseh</u>.

3   Stir up your mighty <u>strength</u>
     and come to our sal<u>vation</u>.
4   Turn us again, O <u>God</u>;
     show the light of your countenance, and we shall be <u>saved</u>.

5   O Lord God of <u>hosts</u>,
     how long will you be angry at your people's <u>prayer</u>?
6   You feed them with the bread of <u>tears</u>;
     you give them abundance of tears to <u>drink</u>.

7   You have made us the derision of our <u>neighbours</u>,
     and our enemies laugh us to <u>scorn</u>.
8   Turn us again, O Lord God of <u>hosts</u>;
     show the light of your countenance, and we shall be <u>saved</u>.

18   Let your hand be upon the man at your <u>right hand</u>,
       the son of man you made so strong for your<u>self</u>.
19   And so will we not go back from <u>you</u>;
       give us life, and we shall call upon your <u>name</u>.

Christmas Day–Epiphany 1

see Years B & C

Epiphany 2

Ps 40 v.1-12

R v.1

AJC

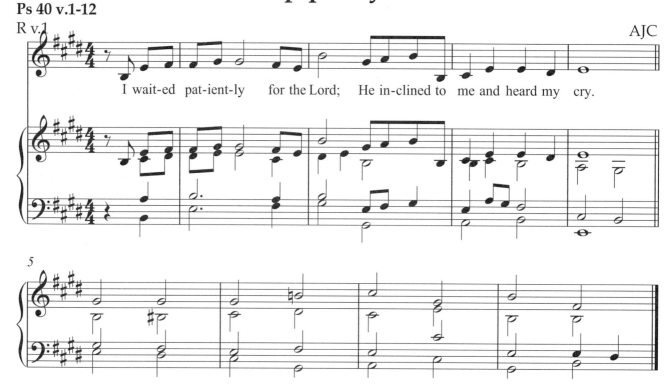

I wait-ed pat-ient-ly for the Lord; He in-clined to me and heard my cry.

I waited patiently for the Lord; he inclined to me and heard my cry.

2   He brought me out of the roaring pit, out of the mire and <u>clay</u>;
    he set my feet upon a rock and made my footing <u>sure</u>.
3   He has put a new song in my mouth, a song of praise to our <u>God</u>;
    many shall see and fear and put their trust in the <u>Lord</u>.

4   Blessed is the one who trusts in the <u>Lord</u>,
    who does not turn to the proud that follow a <u>lie</u>.
5   Great are the wonders you have done, O Lord my God. How great your de<u>signs for us</u>!
    There is none that can be compared with <u>you</u>.

6   If I were to proclaim them and <u>tell of them</u>
    they would be more than I am able to ex<u>press</u>.
7   Sacrifice and offering you do not de<u>sire</u>
    but my ears you have <u>opened</u>;

8   Burnt offering and sacrifice for sin you have not re<u>quired</u>;
    then said I: 'Lo, I <u>come</u>.
9   'In the scroll of the book it is written of me that I should do your will, O my <u>God</u>;
    I delight to do it: your law is within my <u>heart</u>.'

10   I have declared your righteousness in the great congre<u>gation</u>;
    behold, I did not restrain my <u>lips</u>,
    and that, O Lord, you <u>know</u>.
11   Your righteousness I have not hidden in my <u>heart</u>;

11a I have spoken of your faithfulness and your sal<u>vation</u>;
    I have not concealed your loving-kindness and truth from the great congre<u>gation</u>.
12   Do not withhold your compassion from me, O <u>Lord</u>;
    let your love and your faithfulness always pre<u>serve</u> me.

Epiphany 3

Ps 27 v.1, 4-12

R v.1a

The Lord is my light and my salvation; whom then shall I fear?

1b The Lord is the strength of | my life
of whom then shall I | be afraid?

4 One thing have I asked of the Lord and that a|lone I seek:
that I may dwell in the house of the Lord all the days | of my life,

5 To behold the fair beauty of | the Lord
and to seek his will | in his temple.

6 For in the day of trouble he shall hide me | in his shelter;
in the secret place of his dwelling shall he hide me and set me high up|on a rock.

7 And now shall he lift up | my head
above my enemies | round about me;

8 Therefore will I offer in his dwelling an oblation with | grëat gladness;
I will sing and make music | to the Lord.

9 Hear my voice O Lord when | I call;
have mercy u|pon me and answer me.

10 My heart tells of your word | 'Seek my face.'
Your face Lord | will I seek.

11 Hide not your face | from me,
nor cast your servant away | in displeasure.

12 You have | been my helper;
leave me not neither forsake me O God of | my salvation.

Epiphany 4

Ps. 15
R. v. 1

AJC

Lord, who may dwell in your tabernacle?
Who may rest upon your holy hill?

1   Lord, who may dwell in your <u>tabernacle</u>?
     Who may rest upon your holy <u>hill</u>?
2   Whoever leads an uncorrupt <u>life</u>
     and does the thing that is <u>right</u>;

3   Who speaks the truth from the <u>heart</u>
     and bears no deceit on the <u>tongue</u>;
4   Who does no evil to a <u>friend</u>
     and pours no scorn on a <u>neighbour</u>;

5   In whose sight the wicked are not es<u>teemed</u>,
     but who honours those who fear the <u>Lord</u>.
6   Whoever has sworn to a <u>neighbour</u>
     and never goes back on that <u>word</u>;

7   Who does not lend money in hope of <u>gain</u>,
     nor takes a bribe against the <u>innocent</u>;
8   Whoever does these <u>things</u>
     shall never <u>fall</u>.

Candlemas
see Years B & C

Proper 0

Ps 112 v.1-9

R v.1

PT

Alleluia. Blessed are those who fear the Lord
and have great delight in his commandments.

2   Their descendants will be mighty in | the land,
     a generation of the faithful that | will be blest.
3   Wealth and riches will | <u>be in</u> their house,
     and their righteousness en|dures for ever.

4   Light shines in the darkness for | the upright;
     gracious and full of compassion | are the righteous.
5   It goes well with those who are | <u>generous</u> in lending
     and order their af|fairs with justice,

6   For they will never | be shaken;
     the righteous will be held in ever|<u>lasting</u> remembrance.
7   They will not be afraid of any | evil tidings;
     their heart is steadfast trusting | in the Lord.

8   Their heart is sustained and will | not fear,
     until they see the downfall | of their foes.
9   They have given freely to the poor * their righteousness stands | fast for ever;
     their head will be ex|<u>alted</u> with honour.

Proper 1

Ps 119 v.1-8

R. v.1   PT

Bless-ed are those whose way is pure, who walk in the law of the Lord.

Blessed are those whose way is pure,
who walk in the law of the Lord.

2   Blessed are those who keep | his testimonies
     and seek him | with their whole heart,
3   Those who do no wickedness * but walk | in his ways.
4   You O Lord have charged that we should diligently keep | your commandments.

5   O that my ways were made so | direct
     that I might | keep your statutes.
6   Then should I not be | put to shame,
     because I have regard for all | your commandments.

7   I will thank you with an un|feigned heart,
     when I have learned your | righteous judgements.
8   I will | keep your statutes;
     O forsake me | nöt utterly.

Proper 2

Ps 119 v.33-40
R v.33
AJC

Teach me, O Lord, the way of your statutes and I shall keep it to the end.

33 Teach me, O Lord, the way of your <u>statutes</u>
    and I shall keep it to the <u>end</u>.
34 Give me understanding and I shall keep your <u>law</u>;
    I shall keep it with my <u>whole heart</u>.

35 Lead me in the path of your com<u>mandments</u>,
    for therein is my de<u>light</u>.
36 Incline my heart to your <u>testimonies</u>
    and not to unjust <u>gain</u>.

37 Turn away my eyes lest they gaze on <u>vanities</u>;
    O give me life in your <u>ways</u>.
38 Confirm to your servant your <u>promise</u>,
    which stands for all who <u>fear you</u>.

39 Turn away the reproach which I <u>dread</u>,
    because your judgements are <u>good</u>.
40 Behold, I long for your com<u>mandments</u>;
    in your righteousness give me <u>life</u>.

The Second Sunday before Lent

Option A

Ps 136 v.1-9 (23-26)

R v.1

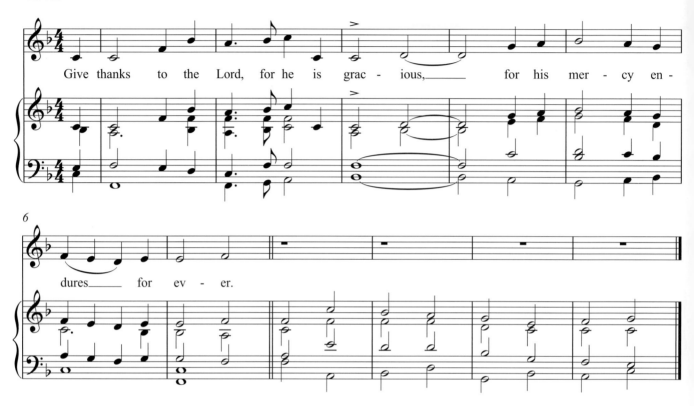

Give thanks to the Lord, for he is gracious,_____ for his mer - cy en -

dures_____ for ev - er.

Give thanks to the Lord, for he is gracious, for his mercy endures for ever.

2   Give thanks to the God of <u>gods</u>,
for his mercy endures for <u>ever</u>.

3   Give thanks to the Lord of <u>lords</u>,
for his mercy endures for <u>ever</u>.

4   Who alone does great <u>wonders</u>,
for his mercy endures for <u>ever</u>.

5   Who by wisdom made the <u>heavens</u>,
for his mercy endures for <u>ever</u>.

6   Who laid out the earth upon the <u>waters</u>,
for his mercy endures for <u>ever</u>.

7   Who made the great <u>lights</u>,
for his mercy endures for <u>ever</u>.

8   The sun to rule the <u>day</u>,
for his mercy endures for <u>ever</u>.

9   The moon and the stars to govern the <u>night</u>,
for his mercy endures for <u>ever</u>.

23   Who remembered us when we were in <u>trouble</u>,
for his mercy endures for <u>ever</u>.

24   And delivered us from our <u>enemies</u>,
for his mercy endures for <u>ever</u>;

25   Who gives food to all <u>creatures</u>,
for his mercy endures for <u>ever</u>.

26   Give thanks to the God of <u>heaven</u>,
for his mercy endures for <u>ever</u>.

Proper 3

AJC

I have quieted and stilled my soul.

1   O Lord, my heart is not <u>proud</u>;
     my eyes are not raised in haughty <u>looks</u>.
2   I do not occupy myself with great <u>matters</u>,
     with things that are too <u>high for me</u>.

3   But I have quieted and stilled my soul, like a weaned child on its mother's <u>breast</u>;
     so my soul is quieted with<u>in me</u>.
4   O Israel, trust in the <u>Lord</u>,
     from this time forth for ever<u>more</u>.

The Sunday before Lent

Ps 2
R v 11a-12

AJC

Serve the Lord with fear, _____ and with tremb-ling kiss his feet.

Hap-py are all they _____ who take ref-uge in him. him.

(last time)

Serve the Lord with fear, and with trembling kiss his feet, Happy are all they who take refuge in him.

1 Why are the nations in <u>tu</u>mult,
   and why do the peoples devise a <u>vain plot</u>?
2 The kings of the earth rise up, and the rulers take counsel to<u>gether</u>,
   against the Lord and against his an<u>ointed</u>:
3 'Let us break their bonds a<u>sunder</u>
   and cast away their <u>cords from us</u>.'

4 He who dwells in heaven shall laugh them to <u>scorn</u>;
   the Lord shall have them in de<u>rision</u>.
5 Then shall he speak to them in his wrath and terrify them in his <u>fury</u>:
6 'Yet have I set my king upon my holy hill of <u>Zion</u>.'
7 I will proclaim the decree of the Lord; he <u>said to me</u>:
   'You are my Son; this day have I be<u>gotten you</u>.

8 'Ask of me and I will give you the nations for your in<u>heritance</u>
   and the ends of the earth for your po<u>ssession</u>.
9 'You shall break them with a rod of <u>iron</u>
   and dash them in pieces like a potter's <u>vessel</u>.'
10 Now therefore be wise, O <u>kings</u>;
   be prudent, you judges of the <u>earth</u>.

The Sunday before Lent

Alternative

Ps 99

R. v.1

PT

The Lord is king, let the peo - ple trem- ble, he is en thrn'd a-bove the cher-u- bim, let the earth shake.

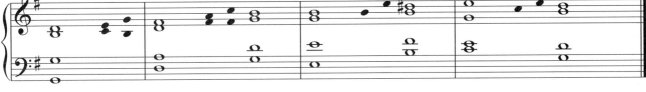

The Lord is king: let the peoples tremble;
he is enthroned above the cherubim: let the earth shake.

2   The Lord is great | in Zion
     and high a|bove all peoples.

3   Let them praise your name, which is | great and awesome;
     the Lord our | God is holy.

4   Mighty king who loves justice * you have estab|lished equity;
     you have executed justice and | <u>righteousness</u> in Jacob.

5   Exalt the | Lord our God;
     bow down before his footstool for | he is holy.

6   Moses and Aaron among his priests *
            and Samuel among those who call upon | his name;
     they called upon the Lord | and he answered them.

7   He spoke to them out of the | <u>pillar</u> of cloud;
     they kept his testimonies and the law | that he gave them.

8   You answered them O Lord | our God;
     you were a God who forgave them and pardoned them for | their offences.

9   Exalt the Lord our God and worship him upon his | holy hill,
     for the Lord our | God is holy.

Ash Wednesday

see Years B & C

Lent 1

Ps 32

R. v.1

Hap-py the one whose trans-gress-ion is for-giv-en, and whose sin is co-vered.

Happy the one whose transgression is forgiven, and whose sin is covered.

2   Happy the one to whom the Lord imputes no guilt * and in whose spirit there is | no guile.

3   For I held my tongue * my bones wasted away through my groaning | all the day long.

4   Your hand was heavy upon me | day and night;
      my moisture was dried up like the | drought in summer.

5   Then I acknowledged | my sin to you
      and my iniquity I | did not hide.

6   I said, 'I will confess my transgressions | to the Lord,'
      and you forgave the guilt | of my sin.

7   Therefore let all the faithful make their prayers to you in time | of trouble;
      in the great water flood it | shall not reach them.

8   You are a place for me to hide in * you pre|serve me from trouble;
      you surround me with | songs of deliverance.

9   'I will instruct you and teach you in the way that you | should go;
      I will guide you | with my eye.

10   'Be not like horse and mule which have | no understanding;
      whose mouths must be held with bit and bridle * or else they will | not stay near you.'

11   Great tribulations remain for | the wicked,
      but mercy embraces those who trust | in the Lord.

12   Be glad you righteous and re|joice in the Lord;
      shout for joy all who are | true of heart.

Lent 2

I lift up my eyes to the hills; from where is my help to come?

1   I lift up my eyes to | the hills;
        from where is my | help to come?
2   My help comes | from the Lord,
        the maker of | <u>heaven</u> and earth.

3   He will not suffer your foot | to stumble;
        he who watches over you | will not sleep.
4   Behold, he who keeps watch | over Israel
        shall neither | <u>slumber</u> nor sleep.

5   The Lord himself wat|ches over you;
        the Lord is your shade | at your right hand,
6   So that the sun shall not | <u>strike you</u> by day,
        neither the | moon by night.

7   The Lord shall keep you from | all evil;
        it is he who shall | keep your soul.
8   The Lord shall keep watch over your going out and your | coming in,
        from this time forth for | evermore.

Lent 3

Ps 95
R v.1

AJC

O come, let us sing to the Lord; let us heart-i-ly re-joice in the rock of our sal-vat-ion.

O come, let us sing to the Lord; let us heartily rejoice in the rock of our salvation.

2   Let us come into his presence with thanks<u>giving</u>
and be glad in him with <u>psalms</u>.

3   For the Lord is a great <u>God</u>
and a great king above all <u>gods</u>.

4   In his hand are the depths of the <u>earth</u>
and the heights of the mountains are his <u>also</u>.

5   The sea is his, for he <u>made it</u>,
and his hands have moulded the dry <u>land</u>.

6   Come, let us worship and bow <u>down</u>
and kneel before the Lord our <u>Maker</u>.

7   For he is our <u>God</u>;
we are the people of his pasture and the sheep of his <u>hand</u>.

8   O that today you would listen to his <u>voice</u>:
'Harden not your hearts as at Meribah, on that day at Massah in the <u>wilderness</u>,

9   'When your forebears tested me, and put me to the <u>proof</u>,
though they had seen my <u>works</u>.

10   'Forty years long I detested that generation and <u>said</u>,
"This people are wayward in their hearts; they do not know my <u>ways</u>."

11   'So I swore in my <u>wrath</u>,
"They shall not enter into my <u>rest</u>." '

Lent 4

Ps. 23
R. v. 1

AJC

The Lord is my shepherd; therefore can I lack nothing.

1   The Lord is my shepherd;
     therefore can I lack nothing.
2   He makes me lie down in green pastures
     and leads me beside still waters.

3   He shall refresh my soul
     and guide me in the paths of righteousness for his name's sake.
4   Though I walk through the valley of the shadow of death, I will fear no evil;
     for you are with me; your rod and your staff, they comfort me.

5   You spread a table before me in the presence of those who trouble me;
     you have anointed my head with oil and my cup shall be full.
6   Surely goodness and loving mercy shall follow me all the days of my life,
     and I will dwell in the house of the Lord for ever.

Mothering Sunday
see Years B & C

Lent 5

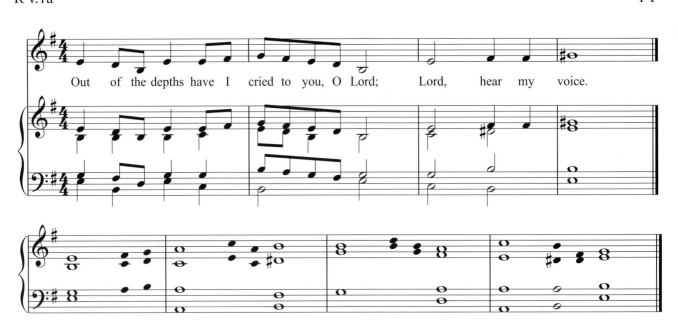

Out of the depths have I cried to you, O Lord; Lord, hear my voice;

1   Out of the depths have I cried to you O Lord * Lord hear | my voice;
     let your ears consider well the voice of my | supplication.
2   If you Lord were to mark what is done amiss * O | Lord who could stand?
3   But there is forgiveness with you * so that | you shall be feared.

4   I wait for the Lord * my | soul waits for him;
     in his | word is my hope.
5   My soul waits for the Lord more than the night watch | for the morning,
     more than the night watch | for the morning.

6   O Israel wait for | the Lord,
     for with the | Lord there is mercy;
7   With him is | plenteous redemption
     and he shall redeem Israel from | all their sins.

Palm Sunday – Easter Day
see Years B & C

Easter 2

Ps. 16
R. v. 10

AJC

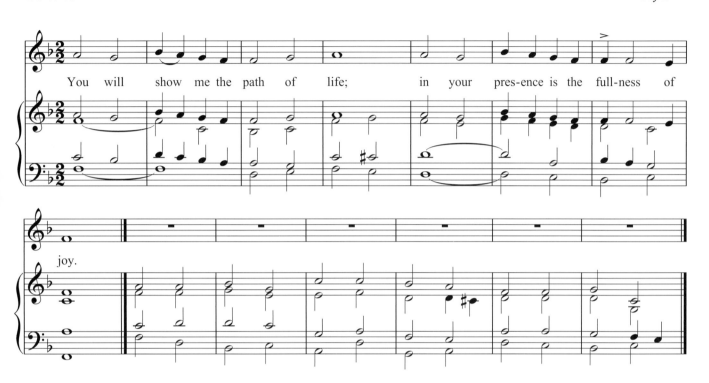

You will   show   me the   path   of   life;   in   your   pres-ence is   the   full-ness   of

joy.

You will show me the path of life; in your presence is the fullness of joy
and in your right hand are pleasures for evermore.

1   Preserve me, O God, for in you have I taken <u>refuge</u>;
       I have said to the Lord, 'You are my lord, all my good depends on <u>you</u>.'
2   All my delight is upon the godly that are in the <u>land</u>,
       upon those who are noble in <u>heart</u>.
3   Though the idols are legion that many run after, their drink offerings of blood I will not <u>offer</u>,
       neither make mention of their names upon my <u>lips</u>.

4   The Lord himself is my portion and my <u>cup</u>;
       in your hands alone is my <u>fortune</u>.
5   My share has fallen in a <u>fair land</u>;
       indeed, I have a goodly <u>heritage</u>.
6   I will bless the Lord who has given me <u>counsel</u>,
       and in the night watches he instructs my <u>heart</u>.

7   I have set the Lord always be<u>fore me</u>;
       he is at my right hand; I shall not <u>fall</u>.
8   Wherefore my heart is glad and my spirit re<u>joices</u>;
       my flesh also shall rest se<u>cure</u>.
9   For you will not abandon my soul to <u>Death</u>,
       nor suffer your faithful one to see the <u>Pit</u>.

Easter 3

I love the Lord, for he has heard the voice of my supplication;
because he inclined his ear to me on the day I called to him.

I love the Lord, for he has heard the voice of my supplication;
because he inclined his ear to me on the day I called to him.

2   The snares of death en<u>compassed me</u>;
       the pains of hell took hold of me; by grief and sorrow was I <u>held</u>.

3   Then I called upon the name of the <u>Lord</u>:
       'O Lord, I beg you, deliver my <u>soul</u>.'

10   How shall I repay the <u>Lord</u>
       for all the benefits he has given to <u>me</u>?

11   I will lift up the cup of sal<u>vation</u>
       and call upon the name of the <u>Lord</u>.

12   I will fulfil my vows to the <u>Lord</u>
       in the presence of all his <u>people</u>.

13   Precious in the sight of the <u>Lord</u>
       is the death of his faithful <u>servants</u>.

14   O Lord, I am your <u>servant</u>,
       your servant the child of your handmaid * you have freed me from my <u>bonds</u>.

15   I will offer to you a sacrifice of <u>thanksgiving</u>
       and call upon the name of the <u>Lord</u>.

16   I will fulfil my vows to the <u>Lord</u>
       in the presence of all his <u>people</u>,

17   In the courts of the house of the <u>Lord</u>,
       in the midst of you, O Jerusalem Alle<u>luia</u>.

Easter 4
see Lent 4

Easter 5

Ps. 31 v.1-4, 15-16
R. v. 16

AJC

Make your face to shine up on your serv - ant,   and   save me for your mer - cy's sake.

'Make your face to shine upon your servant,
and save me for your mercy's sake.'

1   In you, O Lord, have I taken refuge; let me never be put to <u>shame</u>;
     deliver me in your <u>righteousness</u>.
2   Incline your<u> ear to me</u>;
     make haste to de<u>liver me</u>.

3   Be my strong rock, a fortress to save me, for you are my rock and my <u>stronghold</u>;
     guide me, and lead me for your <u>name's sake</u>.
4   Take me out of the net that they have laid secretly <u>for me</u>,
     for you are my <u>strength</u>.

15   'My times are in your <u>hand</u>;
     deliver me from the hand of my enemies, and from those who <u>persecute me</u>.
16   'Make your face to shine upon your <u>servant</u>,
     and save me for your mercy's <u>sake</u>.'

Easter 6

Bless our God, O you peoples; make the voice of his praise to be heard.

7   Bless our God, O you <u>peoples</u>;
      make the voice of his praise to be <u>heard</u>,
8   Who holds our souls in <u>life</u>
      and suffers not our feet to <u>slip</u>.

9   For you, O God, have <u>proved us</u>;
      you have tried us as silver is <u>tried</u>.
10   You brought us into the <u>snare</u>;
      you laid heavy burdens upon our <u>backs</u>.

11   You let enemies ride over our heads; we went through fire and <u>water</u>;
      but you brought us out into a place of <u>liberty</u>.
12   I will come into your house with burnt offerings and will pay you my <u>vows</u>,
      which my lips uttered and my mouth promised when I was in <u>trouble</u>.

13   I will offer you fat burnt sacrifices with the smoke of <u>rams</u>;
      I will sacrifice oxen and <u>goats</u>.
14   Come and listen, all you who fear <u>God</u>,
      and I will tell you what he has done for my <u>soul</u>.

15   I called out to him with my <u>mouth</u>
      and his praise was on my <u>tongue</u>.
16   If I had nursed evil in my <u>heart</u>,
      the Lord would not have <u>heard me</u>,

17   But in truth God has <u>heard me</u>;
      he has heeded the voice of my <u>prayer</u>.
18   Blessed be God, who has not rejected my <u>prayer</u>,
       nor withheld his loving mercy <u>from me</u>.

Ascension Day
see Years B & C

Easter 7
Sunday after the Ascension Day

Ps 68 v.1-10, 32-35

R v.32-33

AJC

D:Sing to God, make mu - sic in praise of the Lord. ___ He

Sing to God, you king-doms of the earth; make mu - sic in praise of the Lord; He

rides on the heavens, and sends forth his voice, a might - y voice.

rides on the anc - ient heav - en of heavens and sends forth his voice, a might - y voice.

Let God arise and let his enemies be <u>scattered</u>;
let those that hate him flee be<u>fore him</u>.
As the smoke vanishes, so may they vanish a<u>way</u>;
as wax melts at the fire, so let the wicked perish
   at the presence of <u>God</u>.
But let the righteous be glad and rejoice before <u>God</u>;
let them make merry with <u>gladness</u>.

Sing to God, sing praises to his name;
   exalt him who rides on the <u>clouds</u>.
The Lord is his name; rejoice be<u>fore him</u>.
Father of the fatherless, defender of <u>widows</u>,
God in his holy habi<u>tation</u>!
God gives the solitary a home and brings forth prisoners
   to songs of <u>welcome</u>,
but the rebellious inhabit a burning <u>desert</u>.

O God, when you went forth before your <u>people</u>,
when you marched through the <u>wilderness</u>,

8   The earth shook and the heavens dropped down rain,
      at the presence of God, the Lord of <u>Sinai</u>,
   at the presence of God, the God of <u>Israel</u>.

9   You sent down a gracious rain, O <u>God</u>;
   you refreshed your inheritance when it was <u>weary</u>.

10   Your people came to <u>dwell there</u>;
   in your goodness, O God, you provide for the <u>poor</u>.

34   Ascribe power to God whose splendour is over <u>Israel</u>,
   whose power is above the <u>clouds</u>.

35   How terrible is God in his holy <u>sanctuary</u>,
   the God of Israel, who gives power and
      strength to his people! Blessed be <u>God</u>.

25

Pentecost

Ps. 104 v.26-36, 37b

R. v.37b

PT

Bless the Lord, O my soul, Al - le - lu - ia, Al - le - lu - ia.

Bless the Lord, O my soul. | Alleluia.

26 O Lord how manifold are | your works!
In wisdom you have made them all * the earth is full | of your creatures.

27 There is the sea spread | far and wide,
and there move creatures beyond number both | small and great.

28 There go the ships * and there is that | Leviathan
which you have made to | play <u>in the</u> deep.

29 All of these look to you to give them their food | in due season.

30 When you give it them they gather it * you open your hand and they are | filled with good.

31 When you hide your face they | are troubled;
when you take away their breath they die and return again | to the dust.

32 When you send forth your spirit they | are created,
and you renew the face | of the earth.

33 May the glory of the Lord endure | for ever;
may the Lord rejoice | in his works;

34 He looks on the earth | and it trembles;
he touches the mountains | and they smoke.

35 I will sing to the Lord as long as | I live;
I will make music to my God while I | have my being.

36 So shall | my song please him
while I rejoice | in the Lord.

Trinity Sunday

Ps 8 *First Version*

R v.1

PT

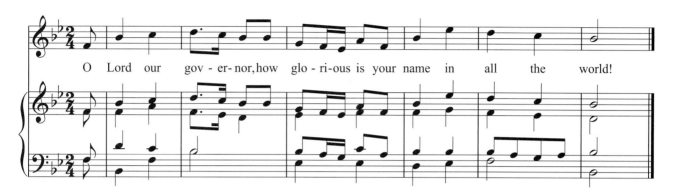

O Lord our gov-er-nor, how glo-ri-ous is your name in all the world!

O Lord our governor,
how glorious is your name in all the world!

2   Your majesty above the heavens | is praised
      out of the mouths of babes | at the breast.

3   You have founded a stronghold a|gainst your foes,
      that you might still the enemy | <u>and the</u> avenger.

4   When I consider your heavens the work of | your fingers,
      the moon and the stars that | <u>you have</u> ordained,

5   What is man that you should be | <u>mindful</u> of him;
      the son of man that you should | seek him out?

6   You have made him little lower than | the angels
      and crown him with | <u>glory</u> and honour.

7   You have given him dominion over the works | of your hands
      and put all things | <u>under</u> his feet,

8   All sheep | and oxen,
      even the wild beasts | of the field,

9   The birds of the air the | <u>fish of</u> the sea
      and whatsoever moves in the paths | of the sea.

Proper 4

Continuous

Ps 46

R v.7

PT

The Lord of hosts is with us; the God of Jacob is our stronghold.

1   God is our refuge | and strength,
        a very present | help in trouble;
2   Therefore we will not fear though the | earth be moved,
        and though the mountains tremble in the | heart of the sea;

3   Though the waters rage | and swell,
        and though the mountains quake at the | towering seas.
4   There is a river whose streams make glad the | city of God,
        the holy place of the dwelling | of the Most High.

5   God is in the midst of her * therefore shall she not be | removed;
        God shall help her at the | break of day.
6   The nations are in uproar and the | kingdoms are shaken,
        but God utters his voice and the earth shall | melt away.

8   Come and behold the works of | the Lord,
        what destruction he has wrought up|on the earth.
9   He makes wars to cease in | all the world;
        he shatters the bow and snaps the spear and burns the chariots | in the fire.

10   'Be still and know that I | am God;
        I will be exalted among the nations * I will be exalted | in the earth.'
11   The Lord of | hosts is with us;
        the God of Jacob | is our stronghold.

Proper 4
Paired

'Make your face to shine upon your servant,
and save me for your mercy's sake.'

1   In you, O Lord, have I taken refuge; let me never be put to <u>shame</u>;
deliver me in your <u>righteousness</u>.

2   Incline your <u>ear to me</u>;
make haste to de<u>liver me</u>.

3   Be my strong rock, a fortress to save me, for you are my rock and my <u>stronghold</u>;
guide me, and lead me for your <u>name's sake</u>.

4   Take me out of the net that they have laid secretly for me, for you are my <u>strength</u>.

5   Into your hands I commend my spirit, for you have redeemed me, O Lord God of <u>truth</u>.

19   How abundant is your goodness, O Lord, which you have laid up for those who <u>fear you</u>;
which you have prepared in the sight of all for those who put their <u>trust in you</u>.

20   You hide them in the shelter of your presence from those who <u>slander them</u>;
you keep them safe in your refuge from the strife of <u>tongues</u>.

21   Blessed be the <u>Lord</u>!
For he has shown me his steadfast love when I was as a city be<u>sieged</u>.

22   I had said in my alarm, 'I have been cut off from the sight of your <u>eyes</u>.'
Nevertheless, you heard the voice of my prayer when I cried <u>out to you.</u>

23   Love the Lord, all you his <u>servants</u>;
for the Lord protects the faithful, but repays to the full the <u>proud</u>.

24   Be strong and let your heart take <u>courage</u>,
all you who wait in hope for the <u>Lord</u>.

Proper 5

Continuous

R. v.1

Rejoice in the Lord, O you righteous,
for it is good for the just to sing praises.

2 Praise the Lord with | the lyre;
   on the ten-stringed harp | sing his praise.
3 Sing for him a new song * play skillfully with | shouts of praise.
4 For the word of the Lord is true * and all his | works are sure.

5 He loves righteousness | and justice;
   the earth is full of the loving-kindness | of the Lord.
6 By the word of the Lord were the | heavens made
   and all their host by the | breath of his mouth.

7 He gathers up the waters of the sea as in | a waterskin
   and lays up the deep | in his treasury.
8 Let all the earth | fear the Lord;
   stand in awe of him, all who | dwell in the world.

9 For he spoke and it | was done;
   he commanded | and it stood fast.
10 The Lord brings the counsel of the | nations to naught;
   he frustrates the designs | of the peoples.

11 But the counsel of the Lord shall endure | for ever
   and the designs of his heart from generation to | generation.
12 Happy the nation whose | God is the Lord
   and the people he has chosen | for his own.

Proper 5

Paired

R. v.15

Call up-on me in the day of trou-ble; I will de - li - ver you and you shall hon - our me.

'Call upon me in the day of trouble;
I will deliver you and you shall honour me.'

7   Hear O my people and I | will speak:
      'I will testify against you O Israel * for I am | God your God.

8   'I will not reprove you | for your sacrifices,
      for your burnt offerings are | <u>always</u> before me.

9   'I will take no bull out of | your house,
      nor he-goat | <u>out of</u> your folds,

10   'For all the beasts of the | <u>forest</u> are mine,
      the cattle upon a | thousand hills.

11   'I know every bird of | the mountains
      and the insect of the | field is mine.

12   'If I were hungry I | would not tell you,
      for the whole world is mine and | all that fills it.

13   'Do you think I eat the flesh | of bulls,
      or drink the | blood of goats?

14   'Offer to God a | <u>sacrifice</u> of thanksgiving
      and fulfil your vows to | God Most High.

Proper 6

Continuous

Ps 116 v.1, 10-17

R v.11

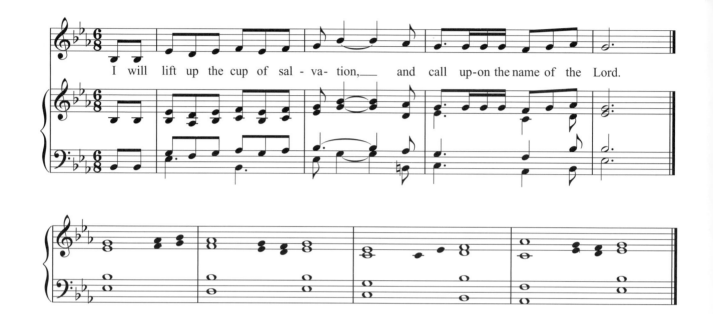

I will lift up the cup of sal - va - tion,___ and call up-on the name of the Lord.

I will lift up the cup of salvation
and call upon the name of the Lord.

1   I love the Lord for he has heard the voice of my supp|lication;
          because he inclined his ear to me on the | day I called to him.
10   How shall I re|pay the Lord
          for all the benefits he has | giv-en to me?

12   I will fulfil my vows to | the Lord
          in the presence of | all his people.
13   Precious in the sight | of the Lord
          is the death of his | faithful servants.

14   O Lord I am | your servant,
          your servant the child of your handmaid * you have freed me | from my bonds.
15   I will offer to you a sacrifice | of thanksgiving
          and call upon the | <u>name of</u> the Lord.

16   I will fulfil my vows to | the Lord
          in the presence of | all his people,
17   In the courts of the | <u>house of</u> the Lord,
          in the midst of you O Jerusalem * | Alleluia.

PT

Proper 6

Paired

O be joyful in the Lord, all the earth.

1   O be joyful in the Lord all | the earth;
    serve the Lord with gladness * and come before his presence | with a song.
2   Know that the | Lord is God;
    it is he that has made us and we are his * we are his people and the | <u>sheep of</u> his pasture.

3   Enter his gates with thanksgiving and his courts | with praise;
    give thanks to him and | bless his name.
4   For the Lord is gracious * his steadfast love is | everlasting,
    and his faithfulness endures from generation to | generation.

Proper 7

Continuous

Ps 86 v.1-10, 16-17

R v.16a

PT

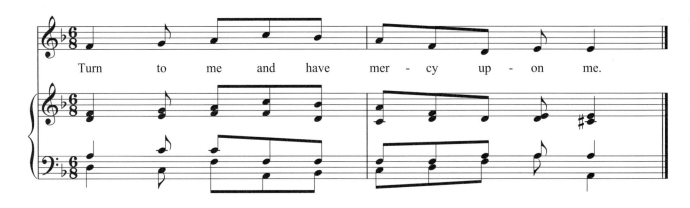

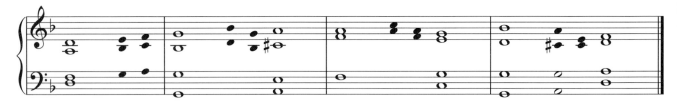

Turn to me and have mercy upon me

1   Incline your ear O Lord | and answer me,
    for I am poor | and in misery.
2   Preserve my soul for | I am faithful;
    save your servant for I | put my trust in you.

3   Be merciful to me O Lord for you are | my God;
    I call upon you | all the day long.
4   Gladden the soul | of your servant,
    for to you O Lord I | lift up my soul.

5   For you Lord are good and | forgiving,
    abounding in steadfast love to all who | call upon you.
6   Give ear O Lord | to my prayer
    and listen to the voice of my | supplication.

7   In the day of my distress I will call | upon you,
    for | you will answer me.
8   Among the gods there is none like | you O Lord,
    nor any | works like yours.

9   All nations you have made shall come and worship you | O Lord,
    and shall glori|fy your name.
10 For you are great and do | wonderful things;
    you a|lone are God.

16 Turn to me and have mercy | upon me;
    give your strength to your servant and save the child | of your handmaid.
17 Show me a token of your favour that those who hate me may see it and | be ashamed;
    because you O Lord have | helped and comforted me.

34

Proper 7
Paired

Ps 69 v.8-11, 18-20
R v.19

AJC

Hide not your face from your servant; be swift to answer me, for I am in trouble.

Bless our God, O you peoples; make the voice of his praise to be heard.

8   For your sake have I suffered re<u>proach</u>;
      shame has covered my <u>face</u>.

9   I have become a stranger to my <u>kindred</u>,
      an alien to my mother's <u>children</u>.

10   Zeal for your house has eaten me <u>up</u>;
      the scorn of those who scorn you has fallen up<u>on me</u>.

11   I humbled myself with <u>fasting</u>,
      but that was turned to my re<u>proach</u>.

18   Answer me, Lord, for your loving-kindness is <u>good</u>;
      turn to me in the multitude of your <u>mercies</u>.

20   Draw near to my soul and re<u>deem me</u>;
      deliver me because of my <u>enemies</u>.

Proper 8

Continuous

Ps 13

R v.6

AJC

I will sing to the Lord, for he has dealt so bountifully with me.

1   How long will you forget me, O Lord; for <u>ev</u>er?
       How long will you hide your <u>face from me</u>?
2   How long shall I have anguish in my soul and grief in my heart, day after <u>day</u>?
       How long shall my enemy triumph <u>over me</u>?

3   Look upon me and answer, O Lord my <u>God</u>;
       lighten my eyes, lest I sleep in <u>death</u>;
4   Lest my enemy say, 'I have prevailed a<u>gainst him</u>,'
       and my foes rejoice that I have <u>fallen</u>.

5   But I put my trust in your steadfast <u>love</u>;
       my heart will rejoice in your sal<u>vation</u>.
6   I will sing to the <u>Lord</u>,
       for he has dealt so bountifully with <u>me</u>.

Proper 8

Paired

Ps 89 v.1-4, 15-18

R v.13

AJC

You have a might-y arm; strong is your hand and high is your right hand.

You have a mighty arm; strong is your hand and high is your right hand.

1. My song shall be always of the loving-kindness of the <u>Lord</u>:
    with my mouth will I proclaim your faithfulness throughout all gene<u>rations</u>.
2. I will declare that your love is established for <u>ever</u>;
    you have set your faithfulness as firm as the <u>heavens</u>.

3. For you said: 'I have made a covenant with my <u>chosen one</u>;
    I have sworn an oath to David my <u>servant</u>:
4. ' "Your seed will I establish for <u>ever</u>
    and build up your throne for all gene<u>rations</u>." '

15. Happy are the people who know the shout of <u>triumph</u>:
    they walk, O Lord, in the light of your <u>countenance</u>.
16. In your name they rejoice all the day <u>long</u>
    and are exalted in your <u>righteousness</u>.

17. For you are the glory of their <u>strength,</u>
    and in your favour you lift up our <u>heads</u>.
18. Truly the Lord is our <u>shield;</u>
    the Holy One of Israel is our <u>king</u>.

37

Proper 9

Continuous

Ps 45 v.10-17

R v.1

AJC

My heart is astir with gracious words;
as I make my song for the king, my tongue is the pen of a ready writer.

10   Hear, O daughter; consider and incline your <u>ear</u>;
     forget your own people and your father's <u>house</u>.
11   So shall the king have pleasure in your <u>beauty</u>;
     he is your lord, so do him <u>honour</u>.

12   The people of Tyre shall bring you <u>gifts</u>;
     the richest of the people shall seek your <u>favour</u>.
13   The king's daughter is all glorious with<u>in</u>;
     her clothing is embroidered cloth of <u>gold</u>.

14   She shall be brought to the king in raiment of <u>needlework</u>;
     after her the virgins that are her com<u>panions</u>.
15   With joy and gladness shall they be <u>brought</u>
     and enter into the palace of the <u>king</u>.

16   'Instead of your fathers you shall have <u>sons</u>,
     whom you shall make princes over all the <u>land</u>.
17   'I will make your name to be remembered through all gener<u>ations</u>;
     therefore shall the peoples praise you for ever and <u>ever</u>.'

Proper 9

Paired

Ps 145 v.8-15

R v.3

AJC

Great   is the Lord   and high-ly   to   be praised;   his _ great-ness is   be - yond all search-ing   out.

3   *Great is the Lord and highly to be praised; his greatness is beyond all searching out.*

8   The Lord is gracious and <u>merciful</u>,
     long-suffering and of great <u>goodness</u>.
9   The Lord is loving to <u>everyone</u>
     and his mercy is over all his <u>creatures</u>.

10   All your works praise you, O <u>Lord</u>,
     and your faithful servants <u>bless you.</u>
11   They tell of the glory of your <u>kingdom</u>
     and speak of your mighty <u>power</u>,

12   To make known to all peoples your mighty <u>acts</u>
     and the glorious splendour of your <u>kingdom</u>.
13   Your kingdom is an everlasting <u>kingdom</u>;
     your dominion endures throughout all <u>ages</u>.

14   The Lord is sure in all his <u>words</u>
     and faithful in all his <u>deeds</u>.
15   The Lord upholds all those who <u>fall</u>
     and lifts up all those who are bowed <u>down</u>.

Proper 10
Continuous

Your word is a lantern to my feet and a light upon my path.

105   Your word is a lantern to my <u>feet</u>
        and a light upon my <u>path</u>.

106   I have sworn and will ful<u>fil it</u>,
        to keep your righteous <u>judgements</u>.

107   I am troubled above <u>measure</u>;
        give me life, O Lord, according to your <u>word</u>.

108   Accept the freewill offering of my mouth, O <u>Lord</u>,
        and teach me your <u>judgements</u>.

109   My soul is ever in my <u>hand</u>,
        yet I do not forget your <u>law</u>.

110   The wicked have laid a <u>snare for me</u>,
        but I have not strayed from your com<u>mandments</u>.

111   Your testimonies have I claimed as my heritage for <u>ever</u>;
        for they are the very joy of my <u>heart</u>.

112   I have applied my heart to fulfil your <u>statutes</u>
        always, even to the <u>end</u>.

Proper 10
Paired

Ps 65 v.(1-7) 8-13

R v.1   PT

Praise is due to you, O God, in Zi-on; to you that ans-wer prayer shall vows be paid.

Praise is due to you, O God, in Zion; to you that answer prayer shall vows be paid.

2   To you shall all flesh come to confess | their sins;
      when our misdeeds prevail against us you will | purge them away.

3   Happy are they whom you choose and draw to your | courts to dwell there.
      We shall be satisfied with the blessings of your house * even of your | holy temple.

4   With wonders you will answer us in your righteousness * O God of our | salvation,
      O hope of all the ends of the earth and of the | farthest seas.

5   In your strength you set | fast the mountains
      and are girded a|bout with might.

6   You still the raging of | the seas,
      the roaring of their waves and the clamour | of the peoples.

7   Those who dwell at the ends of the earth tremble | at your marvels;
      the gates of the morning and evening | sing your praise.

8   You visit the earth | and water it;
      you make it | very plenteous.

9   The river of God is | full of water;
      you prepare grain for your people * for so you provide | for the earth.

10   You drench the furrows and smooth out | the ridges;
      you soften the ground with showers and | bless its increase.

11   You crown the year | with your goodness,
      and your paths over|flow with plenty.

12   May the pastures of the wilderness flow | with goodness
      and the hills be | girded with joy.

13   May the meadows be clothed with | flocks of sheep
      and the valleys stand so thick with corn that they shall | laugh and sing.

Proper 11
Continuous

Ps 139 vv.1-11, 23-24

R. v.1a, c

PT

O Lord, you have searched me out and known me; you discern my thoughts from afar.

1   O Lord, you have searched me out | and known me;
        you know my sitting down and my rising up * you discern my thoughts | from afar.
2   You mark out my journeys | and my resting place
        and are acquainted with | all my ways.

3   For there is not a word on | my tongue,
        but you O Lord know it | altogether.
4   You encompass me behind and before * and lay your | hand upon me.
5   Such knowledge is too wonderful for me * so high that I | cannot attain it.

6   Where can I go then from | your spirit?
        Or where can I flee | from your presence?
7   If I climb up to heaven | you are there;
        if I make the grave my bed | you are there also.

8   If I take the wings of | the morning
        and dwell in the uttermost | parts of the sea,
9   Even there your | hand shall lead me,
        your right hand | hold me fast.

10   If I say 'Surely the darkness | will cover me
        and the light around me | turn to night,'
11   Even darkness is no darkness with you * the night is as | clear as the day;
        darkness and light to you are | both alike.

23   Search me out O God and know | my heart;
        try me and ex|amine my thoughts.
24   See if there is any way of | wickedness in me
        and lead me in the | way everlasting.

Proper 11
Paired

Ps 86 v.11-17

R v.16a

PT

Turn to me and have mercy upon me

11   Teach me your way O Lord and I will walk in | your truth;
        knit my heart to you that I may | fear your name.
12   I will thank you O Lord my God with all my heart *
             and glorify your name for | evermore;
13   For great is your steadfast love towards me *
             for you have delivered my soul from the | <u>depths of</u> the grave.

14   O God the proud rise up against me and a ruthless horde seek after | my life;
        they have not set you be|fore their eyes.
15   But you Lord,are gracious and | <u>full of</u> compassion,
        slow to anger and full of | <u>kindness</u> and truth.

16   Turn to me and have mercy | upon me;
        give your strength to your servant and save the child | of your handmaid.
17   Show me a token of your favour that those who hate me may see it and | be ashamed;
        because you O Lord have | <u>helped</u> and comforted me.

Proper 12

Continuous

Ps 105 v.1-11, 45b

R v. 4

AJC

Seek the Lord and his strength; seek his face continually

1   O give thanks to the Lord and call upon his <u>name</u>;
      make known his deeds among the <u>peoples</u>.
2   Sing to him, sing <u>praises</u>
      and tell of all his marvellous <u>works</u>.

3   Rejoice in the praise of his holy <u>name</u>;
      let the hearts of them rejoice who seek the <u>Lord</u>.
4   Seek the Lord and his <u>strength</u>;
      seek his face con<u>tinually</u>.

5   Remember the marvels he has <u>done</u>,
      his wonders and the judgements of his <u>mouth</u>,
6   O seed of Abraham his <u>servant</u>
      O children of Jacob his <u>chosen</u>.

7   He is the Lord our <u>God</u>;
      his judgements are in all the <u>earth</u>.
8   He has always been mindful of his <u>covenant</u>,
      the promise that he made for a thousand gener<u>ations</u>:

9   The covenant he made with <u>Abraham</u>,
      the oath that he swore to <u>Isaac</u>,
10   Which he established as a statute for <u>Jacob</u>,
      an everlasting covenant for <u>Israel</u>,

11   Saying, 'To you will I give the land of <u>Canaan</u>
      to be the portion of your in<u>heritance</u>.'
45   That they might keep his <u>statutes</u>
      and faithfully observe his laws. Alle<u>luia</u>.

Proper 12
Continuous (Alternative)

Ps 128

R v.1

AJC

Blessed are all those who fear the Lord, and walk in the ways of God.

Blessed are all those who fear the Lord, and walk in the ways of God.

2   You shall eat the fruit of the toil of your <u>hands</u>;
    it shall go well with you, and happy shall you <u>be</u>.
3   Your wife within your house shall be like a fruitful <u>vine</u>;
    your children round your table, like fresh olive <u>branches</u>.

4   Thus shall the one be blest who fears the <u>Lord</u>.
5   The Lord from out of Zion <u>bless you</u>,
    that you may see Jerusalem in prosperity all the days of your <u>life</u>.
6   May you see your children's children, and may there be peace upon <u>Israel</u>.

Proper 12
Paired

Ps 119 v.129-136

R v.130

AJC

The op-ening of your word gives light; it gives un der-stand-ing to the sim - ple.

130   The opening of your word gives light; it gives understanding to the simple.

129   Your testimonies are <u>wonderful</u>;
       therefore my soul <u>keeps them</u>.
130   The opening of your word gives <u>light</u>;
       it gives understanding to the <u>simple</u>.

131   I open my mouth and draw in my <u>breath</u>,
       as I long for your com<u>mandments</u>.
132   Turn to me and be <u>gracious to me</u>,
       as is your way with those who love your <u>name</u>.

133   Order my steps by your <u>word</u>,
       and let no wickedness have dominion <u>over me</u>.
134   Redeem me from earthly op<u>pressors</u>
       so that I may keep your com<u>mandments</u>.

135   Show the light of your countenance upon your <u>servant</u>
       and teach me your <u>statutes</u>.
136   My eyes run down with streams of <u>water</u>,
       because the wicked do not keep your <u>law</u>.

Proper 13

Continuous

Ps. 17 v.1-7, 16

R. v.6a

PT

I call upon you, O God, for you will answer me.

1 Hear my just cause O Lord * consider my | complaint;
listen to my prayer * which comes not from | lying lips.

2 Let my vindication come forth | from your presence;
let your eyes behold | what is right.

3 Weigh my heart, examine me | by night,
refine me and you will find no im|puri-ty in me.

4 My mouth does not trespass for | earthly rewards;
I have heeded the words | of your lips.

5 My footsteps hold fast in the ways of your | commandments;
my feet have not stumbled | in your paths.

6 I call upon you O God for | you will answer me;
incline your ear to me and listen | to my words.

7 Show me your marvellous lov|ing-kindness,
O Saviour of those who take refuge at your right hand from those who rise | up against them.

16 As for me, I shall see your | face in righteousness;
when I awake and behold your likeness | I shall be satisfied.

Proper 13

Paired

Ps 145 v8-9, 16-22

R v.3

AJC

Great is the Lord and highly to be praised; his greatness is beyond all searching out.

8   The Lord is gracious and <u>merciful</u>,
    long-suffering and of great <u>goodness</u>.

9   The Lord is loving to <u>everyone</u>
    and his mercy is over all his <u>creatures</u>.

15   The Lord upholds all those who <u>fall</u>
    and lifts up all those who are bowed <u>down</u>.

16   The eyes of all wait upon you, O <u>Lord</u>,
    and you give them their food in due <u>season</u>.

17   You open wide your <u>hand</u>
    and fill all things living with <u>plenty</u>.

18   The Lord is righteous in all his <u>ways</u>
    and loving in all his <u>works</u>.

19   The Lord is near to those who call up<u>on him</u>,
    to all who call upon him <u>faithfully</u>.

20   He fulfils the desire of those who <u>fear him</u>;
    he hears their cry and <u>saves them</u>.

21   The Lord watches over those who <u>love him</u>,
    but all the wicked shall he de<u>stroy</u>.

22   My mouth shall speak the praise of the <u>Lord</u>,
    and let all flesh bless his holy name for ever and <u>ever</u>.

Proper 14

Continuous

Ps 105 v.1-6, 16-22, 45b

R v.1

PT

O give thanks to the Lord and call upon his name;
make known his deeds among the peoples.

2   Sing to him | sing praises,
      and tell of all his | marvellous works.
3   Rejoice in the praise of his | holy name;
      let the hearts of them rejoice who | seek the Lord.

4   Seek the Lord and his strength * seek his face | continually.
5   Remember the marvels he has done * his wonders and the judgements | of his mouth,
6   O seed of | Abraham his servant,
      O children of | Jacob his chosen.

16   Then he called down famine over the land and broke every staff | of bread.
17   But he had sent a man before them * Joseph who was | sold as a slave.
18   They shackled his feet with fetters * his neck was | ringed with iron.
19   Until all he foretold came to pass * the word of the | Lörd tested him.

20   The king sent and released him * the ruler of peoples set | him free.
21   He appointed him lord of his household and ruler of | all he possessed,
22   To instruct his princes | as he willed
(45b) and to teach his counsellors wisdom * | Alleluia.

49

Proper 14

Paired

R. v. 7

PT

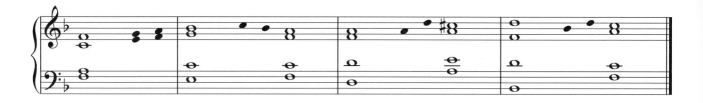

Show us your mercy, O Lord,
and grant us your salvation.

8   I will listen to what the Lord God | will say,
     for he shall speak peace to his people and to the faithful,
          that they turn not a|gain to folly.

9   Truly, his salvation is near to | those who fear him,
          that his glory may dwell | in our land.

10   Mercy and truth are met | together,
     righteousness and peace have | kissed each other;

11   Truth shall spring up | from the earth
     and righteousness look | down from heaven.

12   The Lord will indeed give all that | is good,
     and our land will | yield its increase.

13   Righteousness shall | go before him
     and direct his steps | in the way.

Proper 15

Continuous

Ps 133

R v.1

PT

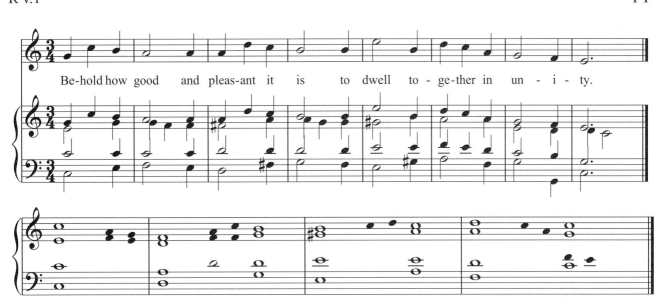

Be-hold how good and pleas-ant it is to dwell to-ge-ther in un - i - ty.

Behold how good and pleasant it is to dwell together in unity.

2   It is like the precious oil upon | the head,
        running down up|on the beard,

3   Even on | Aaron's beard,
        running down upon the collar | of his clothing.

4   It is like the dew | of Hermon
        running down upon the | hills of Zion.

5   For there the Lord has | <u>promised</u> his blessing:
        even life for | evermore.

Proper 15

Paired

Ps 67

R v.3

PT

Let the peo - ples praise you, O God; let all the peo - ples praise you.

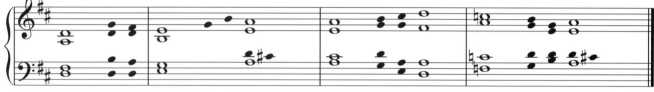

Let the peoples praise you, O God; let all the peoples praise you.

1   God be gracious to us | and bless us
     and make his face to | shine upon us,
2   That your way may be | <u>known up</u>on earth,
     your saving power a|mong all nations.

4   O let | the nations
     rejoice | and be glad,
     for you will judge the | peoples righteously
     and govern the nations | upon earth.

6   Then shall the earth bring forth | her increase,
     and God our own | God will bless us.
7   God | will bless us,
     and all the ends of the | earth shall fear him.

Proper 16

Continuous

Ps 124

R v.3

AJC

Our help is in the name of the Lord, who has made heaven and earth.

1   If the Lord himself had not been on our <u>side,</u>
            now may Israel <u>say</u>;

2   If the Lord had not been on our <u>side,</u>
            when enemies rose up a<u>gainst us</u>;

3   Then would they have swallowed us a<u>live</u>
            when their anger burned a<u>gainst us</u>;

4   Then would the waters have overwhelmed us and the torrent gone over our <u>soul</u>;
            over our soul would have swept the raging <u>waters</u>.

5   But blessed be the <u>Lord</u>
            who has not given us over to be a prey for their <u>teeth</u>.

6   Our soul has escaped as a bird from the snare of the <u>fowler</u>;
            the snare is broken and we are de<u>livered</u>.

Proper 16

Paired

Ps 138

R. v3

AJC

In the day that I called to you, you answered me; you put new strength in my soul.

1   I will give thanks to you, O Lord, with my whole heart;
           before the gods will I sing praise to you.
2   I will bow down towards your holy temple and praise your name, *
           because of your love and faithfulness;
    for you have glorified your name and your word above all things.

4   All the kings of the earth shall praise you, O Lord, *
           for they have heard the words of your mouth.
5   They shall sing of the ways of the Lord, *
           that great is the glory of the Lord.
6   Though the Lord be high, he watches over the lowly;
    as for the proud, he regards them from afar.

7   Though I walk in the midst of trouble, you will preserve me;
    you will stretch forth your hand against the fury of my enemies; *
           your right hand will save me.
8   The Lord shall make good his purpose for me;
    your loving-kindness, O Lord, endures for ever; *
           forsake not the work of your hands.

Proper 17

Continuous

Ps 105 v.1-6, 23-26, 45c

R v.4

AJC

Seek the — Lord and his strength; seek his face con - tin - ual - ly.

Seek the Lord and his strength; seek his face continually.

1   O give thanks to the Lord and call upon his <u>name</u>;
        make known his deeds among the <u>peoples</u>.

2   Sing to him, sing <u>praises</u>
        and tell of all his marvellous <u>works</u>.

3   Rejoice in the praise of his holy <u>name</u>;
        let the hearts of them rejoice who seek the <u>Lord</u>.

4   Seek the Lord and his <u>strength</u>;
        seek his face con<u>tinually</u>.

5   Remember the marvels he has <u>done</u>,
        his wonders and the judgements of his <u>mouth</u>,

6   O seed of Abraham his <u>servant</u>,
        O children of Jacob his <u>chosen</u>.

23   Then Israel came into <u>Egypt</u>;
        Jacob sojourned in the land of <u>Ham</u>.

24   And the Lord made his people exceedingly <u>fruitful</u>;
        he made them too many for their <u>adversaries</u>,

25   Whose heart he turned, so that they hated his <u>people</u>
        and dealt craftily with his <u>servants</u>.

26   Then sent he Moses his <u>servant</u>

45c   and Aaron whom he had chosen. Alle<u>luia</u>.

Proper 17
Continuous (Alternative)

Ps. 115

R v. 1

AJC

Not to us, Lord, not to us, but to your name give the glory, for the sake of your loving mercy and truth.

2 Why should the nations <u>say</u>,
 'Where is now their <u>God</u>?'

3 As for our God, he is in <u>heaven</u>;
 he does whatever he <u>pleases</u>.

4 Their idols are silver and <u>gold</u>,
 the work of human <u>hands</u>.

5 They have mouths, but cannot <u>speak</u>;
 eyes have they, but cannot <u>see</u>;

6 They have ears, but cannot <u>hear</u>;
 noses have they, but cannot <u>smell</u>;

7 They have hands, but cannot feel;
 feet have they, but cannot <u>walk</u>;
 not a whisper do they make from their <u>throats</u>.

8 Those who make them shall be<u>come like them</u>
 and so will all who put their <u>trust in them</u>.

9 But you, Israel, put your trust in the <u>Lord</u>;
 he is their help and their <u>shield</u>.

10 House of Aaron, trust in the <u>Lord</u>;
 he is their help and their <u>shield</u>.

11 You that fear the Lord, trust in the <u>Lord</u>;
 he is their help and their <u>shield</u>.

12 The Lord has been mindful of us
 and he will <u>bless us</u>;
 may he bless the house of Israel;
 may he bless the house of <u>Aaron</u>;

13 May he bless those who fear the <u>Lord</u>,
 both small and great to<u>gether</u>.

14 May the Lord increase you more and more,
 you and your children <u>after you</u>.

15 May you be blest by the Lord,
 the maker of heaven and <u>earth</u>.

16 The heavens are the heavens of the <u>Lord</u>,
 but the earth he has entrusted to his <u>children</u>.

17 The dead do not praise the <u>Lord</u>,
 nor those gone down into <u>silence</u>;

18 But we will bless the <u>Lord</u>,
 from this time forth for evermore. Alle<u>luia</u>.

Proper 17
Paired

My foot stands firm; in the great congregation I will bless the Lord.

1   Give judgement for me, O Lord, for I have walked with in<u>tegrity</u>;
      I have trusted in the Lord and have not <u>faltered</u>.

2   Test me, O Lord, and <u>try me</u>;
      examine my heart and my <u>mind</u>.

3   For your love is before my <u>eyes</u>;
      I have walked in your <u>truth</u>.

4   I have not joined the company of the <u>false</u>,
      nor consorted with the de<u>ceitful</u>.

5   I hate the gathering of <u>evildoers</u>
      and I will not sit down with the <u>wicked</u>.

6   I will wash my hands in innocence, O <u>Lord</u>,
      that I may go about your <u>altar</u>,

7   To make heard the voice of <u>thanksgiving</u>
      and tell of all your wonderful <u>deeds</u>.

8   Lord, I love the house of your habi<u>tation</u>
      and the place where your glory a<u>bides</u>.

Proper 18

Continuous

R v.1

PT

Al - le - lu - ia. O sing to the Lord a new song; sing his praise in the con-gre- ga - tion of the faith- ful.

Alleluia. O sing to the Lord a new song;
sing his praise in the congregation of the faithful.

2   Let Israel rejoice in | their maker;
     let the children of Zion be joyful | in their king.
3   Let them praise his | name in the dance;
     let them sing praise to him with | timbrel and lyre.

4   For the Lord has pleasure in | his people
     and adorns the | poor with salvation.
5   Let the faithful be | joyful in glory;
     let them | rejoice in their ranks,

6   With the praises of God in | their mouths
     and a two-edged | sword in their hands;
7   To execute vengeance | on the nations
     and punishment | on the peoples;

8   To bind their kings | in chains
     and their nobles with | fetters of iron;
9   To execute on them the | judgement decreed:
     such honour have all his faithful servants * | Alleluia.

Proper 18 Paired

See Proper 2

Proper 19

Continuous

Ps 114
R v.7a

PT

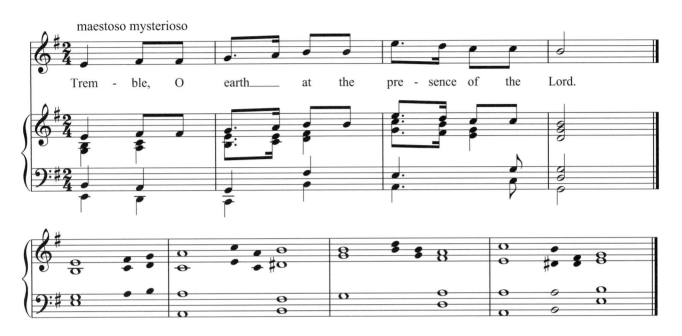

Tremble, O earth, at the presence of the Lord

1   When Israel came out | of Egypt,
        the house of Jacob from a people | of a strange tongue,
2   Judah be|came his sanctuary,
        Israel | his dominion.

3   The sea saw that | and fled;
        Jordan was | driven back.
4   The mountains | skipped like rams,
        the little hills | like young sheep.

5   What ailed you O sea that | you fled?
        O Jordan that you were | driven back?
6   You mountains that you | skipped like rams,
        you little hills | like young sheep?

7   Tremble O earth at the presence of | the Lord,
        at the presence of the | God of Jacob,
8   Who turns the hard rock into a | pool of water,
        the flint-stone into a | springing well.

Proper 19

Paired

Ps. 103 v. (1-7), 8-13

R. v. 1

Bless the Lord, O my soul, and all that is within me bless his holy name.

[2   Bless the Lord, O my soul, and forget not all | his benefits;

3   Who forgives all your sins and heals all | your infirmities;

4   Who redeems your life from the Pit *
         and crowns you with faithful love | and compassion;

5   Who satisfies you with good things *
     so that your youth is renewed | like an eagle's.]

[6   The Lord executes righteousness | and judgement
     for all who | are oppressed.

7   He made his ways | known to Moses
     and his works to the | children of Israel.]

8   The Lord is full of compassion | and mercy,
     slow to anger and of | grëat kindness.

9   He will not | always accuse us,
     neither will he keep his | anger for ever.

10   He has not dealt with us according to | our sins,
     nor rewarded us according | to our wickedness.

11   For as the heavens are high a|bove the earth,
     so great is his mercy upon | those who fear him.

12   As far as the east is from | the west,
     so far has he | set our sins from us.

13   As a father has compassion | on his children,
     so is the Lord merciful towards | those who fear him.

Proper 20

Continuous

Ps 105 v.1-6, 37-45

R v.1

O give thanks to the Lord and call up-on his name; make known his deeds a-mong the peo - ples.

O give thanks to the Lord and call upon his name;
make known his deeds among the peoples.

2   Sing to him | sing praises,
     and tell of all his | marvellous works.
3   Rejoice in the praise of his | holy name;
     let the hearts of them rejoice who | seek the Lord.

4   Seek the Lord and his strength * seek his face | continually.
5   Remember the marvels he has done * his wonders and the judgements | of his mouth,
6   O seed of | Abraham his servant,
     O children of | Jacob his chosen.

37   Then he brought them out with silver and gold *
             there was not one among their tribes | that stumbled.
38   Egypt was glad at their departing, for a dread of them had | fallen upon them.
39   He spread out a cloud | for a covering
     and a fire to | light up the night.

40   They asked and he brought | them quails;
     he satisfied them with the | bread of heaven.
41   He opened the rock and the | waters gushed out
     and ran in the dry places | like a river.

42   For he remembered his ho|ly word
     and Abra|ham his servant.
43   So he brought forth his | people with joy,
     his chosen | ones with singing.

44   He gave them the lands of | the nations
     and they took possession of the | fruit of their toil,
45   That they might | keep his statutes
     and faithfully observe his laws. | Alleluia.

61

Proper 20

Paired

Great is the Lord and high-ly to be praised; his _ great-ness is be-yond all search-ing out.

1   I will exalt you, O God my <u>King</u>,
     and bless your name for ever and <u>ever</u>.
2   Every day will I <u>bless you</u>
     and praise your name for ever and <u>ever</u>.

4   One generation shall praise your works to <u>another</u>
     and declare your mighty <u>acts</u>.
5   They shall speak of the majesty of your <u>glory</u>,
     and I will tell of all your wonderful <u>deeds</u>.

6   They shall speak of the might of your marvellous <u>acts</u>,
     and I will also tell of your <u>greatness</u>.
7   They shall pour forth the story of your abundant kindness
          and joyfully sing of your <u>righteousness</u>.
8   The Lord is gracious and merciful, long-suffering and of great <u>goodness</u>.

Proper 21

Continuous

Ps 78 v.1-4, 12-16

R v.1b

Incline your ears to the words of my mouth.

1   Hear my teaching O | my people;
     incline your ears to the words | of my mouth.
2   I will open my mouth | in a parable;
     I will pour forth mysteries | from of old,

3   Such as we have heard | and known,
     which our | forebears have told us.
4   We will not hide from their children but will recount to gener|ations to come,
     the praises of the Lord and his power and the wonderful works | he has done.

12   For he did marvellous things in the sight of | their forebears,
     in the land of Egypt in the | field of Zoan.
13   He divided the sea and | let them pass through;
     he made the waters stand still | in a heap.

14   He led them with a cloud by day and all the night through with a blaze | of fire.
15   He split the hard rocks in the wilderness and gave them drink as | from the great deep.
16   He brought streams | out of the rock
     and made water | gush out like rivers.

Proper 21
Paired

Remember, Lord your com - pas - sion and love, for they are from e - ver - last - ing.

Remember, Lord, your compassion and love,
for they are from everlasting.

1   To you, O Lord, I lift up my soul; O my God, in you | I trust;
     let me not be put to shame; let not my enemies | triumph over me.
2   Let none who look to you be | put to shame,
     but let the treacherous be shamed | and frustrated.

3   Make me to know your ways, | O Lord,
     and teach | me your paths.
4   Lead me in your truth and teach me, for you are the God of | my salvation;
     for you have I hoped | all the day long.

6   Remember not the sins of | my youth
     or | my transgressions,
     but think on me in your | goodness, O Lord,
     according to your | steadfast love.

7   Gracious and upright is | the Lord;
     therefore shall he teach sinners | in the way.
8   He will guide the humble in | doing right
     and teach his way | to the lowly.

Proper 22

Continuous

Ps 19

R v14

AJC

Let the words of my mouth and the med-i-ta-tion of my heart be ac-cept-ab-le in your sight, O Lord my strength and my re-deem-er.

1   The heavens are telling the glory of <u>God</u>
     and the firmament proclaims his <u>handiwork</u>.

2   One day pours out its song to an<u>other</u>
     and one night unfolds knowledge to an<u>other</u>.

3   They have neither speech nor <u>language</u>
     and their voices are not <u>heard</u>,

4   Yet their sound has gone out into <u>all lands</u>
     and their words to the ends of the <u>world</u>.

5   In them has he set a tabernacle for the <u>sun</u>,
     that comes forth as a bridegroom out of his chamber *
         and rejoices as a champion to run his <u>course</u>.

6   It goes forth from the end of the heavens *
         and runs to the very end a<u>gain</u>,
   and there is nothing hidden from its <u>heat</u>.

7   The law of the Lord is perfect, reviving the <u>soul</u>;
     the testimony of the Lord is sure and gives wisdom to the <u>simple</u>.

8   The statutes of the Lord are right and rejoice the <u>heart</u>;
     the commandment of the Lord is pure and gives light to the <u>eyes</u>.

9   The fear of the Lord is clean and endures for <u>ever</u>;
     the judgements of the Lord are true and righteous alto<u>gether</u>.

10   More to be desired are they than gold, more than much fine <u>gold</u>,
     sweeter also than honey, dripping from the <u>honeycomb</u>.

11   By them also is your servant <u>taught</u>
     and in keeping them there is great re<u>ward</u>.

12   Who can tell how often they of<u>fend</u>?
     O cleanse me from my secret <u>faults</u>!

13   Keep your servant also from presumptuous sins *
         lest they get dominion <u>over me</u>;
   so shall I be undefiled, and innocent of great of<u>fence</u>.

14   Let the words of my mouth and the meditation
         of my heart be acceptable in your <u>sight</u>,
   O Lord, my strength and my re<u>deemer</u>.

65

Proper 22

Paired

Ps 80 v.1-6

R v 4

AJC

Turn us again, O God of hosts;
show the light of your countenance, and we shall be saved.

1   Hear, O Shepherd of <u>Is</u>rael,
    you that led Joseph like a <u>flock</u>;
2   Shine forth, you that are enthroned upon the <u>che</u>rubim,
    before Ephraim, Benjamin and Man<u>as</u>seh.

3   Stir up your mighty <u>strength</u>
    and come to our sal<u>va</u>tion.
4   Turn us again, O <u>God</u>;
    show the light of your countenance, and we shall be <u>saved</u>.

5   O Lord God of <u>hosts</u>,
    how long will you be angry at your people's <u>prayer</u>?
6   You feed them with the bread of <u>tears</u>;
    you give them abundance of tears to <u>drink</u>.

Proper 23

Continuous

Ps 106 v.1-6, 19-23

R v 1

AJC

Give thanks to the Lord, for he is gracious, for his faithfulness endures for ever.

2   Who can express the mighty acts of the <u>Lord</u>
       or show forth all his <u>praise</u>?

3   Blessed are those who observe what is <u>right</u>
       and always do what is <u>just</u>.

4   Remember me, O Lord, in the favour you bear for your <u>people</u>;
       visit me in the day of your sal<u>vation</u>;

5   That I may see the prosperity of your chosen and rejoice in the gladness of your <u>people</u>,
       and exult with your in<u>heritance</u>.

6   We have sinned like our <u>forebears</u>;
       we have done wrong and dealt <u>wickedly</u>.

19   They made a calf at Horeb and worshipped the molten <u>image</u>;

20   Thus they exchanged their glory for the image of an ox that feeds on <u>hay</u>.

21   They forgot God their saviour, who had done such great things in <u>Egypt</u>,

22   Wonderful deeds in the land of Ham and fearful things at the <u>Red Sea</u>.

23   So he would have destroyed them, had not Moses his chosen stood before him in the <u>breach</u>,
       to turn away his wrath from con<u>suming them</u>.

Proper 23 Paired
see Lent 4

Proper 24 Continuous
see 1 before Lent

Proper 24
Paired

Ps 96 v.1-9 (10-13)

R v.1

PT

Sing to the Lord a new song; sing to the Lord all the earth.

Sing to the Lord a new song; sing to the Lord all the earth.

2   Sing to the Lord and bless | his name
        tell out his salvation from | day to day.

3   Declare his glory a|mong the nations
        and his wonders a|mong all peoples.

4   For great is the Lord and greatly to | be praised;
        he is more to be feared | than all gods.

5   For all the gods of the nations | are but idols;
        it is the Lord who | made the heavens.

6   Honour and majesty are | before him;
        power and splendour are | in his sanctuary.

7   Ascribe to the Lord you families | of the peoples;
        ascribe to the Lord | <u>honour</u> and strength.

8   Ascribe to the Lord the honour due to | his name;
        bring offerings and come | <u>into</u> his courts.

9   O worship the Lord in the | <u>beauty</u> of holiness;
        let the whole earth | <u>tremble</u> before him.

[10   Tell it out among the nations that the Lord | is king.
        He has made the world so firm that it cannot be moved *he will judge the | <u>peoples</u> with equity.

11   Let the heavens rejoice and let the | earth be glad;
        let the sea thunder and | <u>all that</u> is in it;

12   Let the fields be joyful and all that | is in them;
        let all the trees of the wood shout for joy be|fore the Lord.

13   For he comes, he comes to | judge the earth;
        with righteousness he will judge the world * and the peoples | with his truth.]

Proper 25
Continuous

Ps 90 v.1-6, 13-17

R v.17

AJC

May the gracious favour of the Lord our God be upon us

1   Lord, you have been our <u>refuge</u>
   from one generation to an<u>other</u>.
2   Before the mountains were brought forth, or the earth and the world were <u>formed</u>,
   from everlasting to everlasting you are <u>God</u>.

3   You turn us back to dust and <u>say</u>:
   'Turn back, O children of <u>earth</u>.'
4   For a thousand years in your sight are but as <u>yesterday</u>,
   which passes like a watch in the <u>night</u>.

5   You sweep them away like a <u>dream</u>;
   they fade away suddenly like the <u>grass</u>.
6   In the morning it is green and <u>flourishes</u>;
   in the evening it is dried up and <u>withered</u>.

13 Turn again, O Lord; how long will you de<u>lay</u>?
   Have compassion on your <u>servants</u>.
14 Satisfy us with your loving-kindness in the <u>morning</u>,
   that we may rejoice and be glad all our <u>days</u>.

15 Give us gladness for the days you have af<u>flicted us</u>,
   and for the years in which we have seen ad<u>versity</u>.
16 Show your servants your <u>works</u>,
   and let your glory be over their <u>children</u>.

Proper 25
Paired

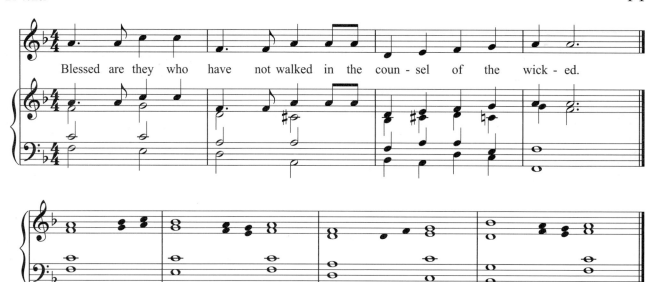

Blessed are they who have not walked in the coun - sel of the wick - ed.

Blessed are they who have not walked in the counsel of the wicked.

1   Blessed are they who have not walked in the counsel of | the wicked,
     nor lingered in the way of sinners * nor sat in the assembly | of the scornful.

2   Their delight is in the | law of the Lord
     and they meditate on his law | day and night.

3   Like a tree planted by streams of water bearing fruit in due season *
            with leaves that do | not wither,
     whatever they do | it shall prosper.

4   As for the wicked it is not | so with them;
     they are like chaff which the wind | blows away.

5   Therefore the wicked shall not be able to stand in | the judgement,
     nor the sinner in the congregation | of the righteous.

6   For the Lord knows the way | of the righteous,
     but the way of the | wicked shall perish.

Proper 26

Continuous

Ps. 107 v. 1-7, 33-37

R. v. 1

O give thanks to the Lord, for he is gra-cious, for his stead-fast love en-dures for ev - er.

O give thanks to the Lord, for he is gracious, for his steadfast love endures for ever.

2   Let the redeemed of the Lord | say this,
     those he redeemed from the hand | of the enemy,
3   And gathered out of the lands from the east and | from the west,
     from the north and | from the south.

4   Some went astray in de|sert wastes
     and found no path to a | city to dwell in.
5   Hun|gry and thirsty,
     their soul was | fainting within them.

6   So they cried to the Lord in | their trouble
     and he delivered them from | their distress.
7   He set their feet | on the right way
     till they came to a | city to dwell in.

33   The Lord turns rivers in|to wilderness
     and water springs into | thirsty ground;
34   A fruitful land he makes a | salty waste,
     because of the wickedness of | those who dwell there.

35   He makes the wilderness a pool | of water
     and water springs out of a | thirsty land.
36   There he settles the hungry and they build a | city to dwell in.
37   They sow fields and plant vineyards and bring in a | fruitful harvest.

Proper 26

Paired

O put your trust in God, for I will yet give him thanks who is the

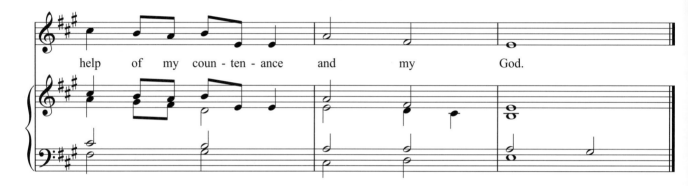

help of my coun - ten - ance and my God.

O put your trust in God, for I will yet give him thanks,
who is the help of my countenance and my God.

1   Give judgement for me O God and defend my cause against an ungod|ly people;
     deliver me from the deceitful | and the wicked.
2   For you are the God of my refuge * why have you | cast me from you,
     and why go I so heavily while the | <u>enemy</u> oppresses me?

3   O send out your light and your truth that they | may lead me,
     and bring me to your holy hill and | to your dwelling,
4   That I may go to the altar of God * to the God of my | joy and gladness;
     and on the lyre I will give thanks to you O | God my God.

5   Why are you so full of heaviness O | my soul,
     and why are you so dis|<u>quieted</u> within me?
6   O put your | trust in God;
     for I will yet give him thanks who is the help of my countenance | and my God.

All Saints

Ps. 34 v. 1-10

R. v. 8

PT

O taste and see that the Lord is gra cious; bless'd is the one who trusts in him.

O taste and see that the Lord is gracious;
blessed is the one who trusts in him.

1   I will bless the Lord | at all times;
    his praise shall ever be | in my mouth.

2   My soul shall glory | in the Lord;
    let the humble hear | and be glad.

3   O magnify the Lord | with me;
    let us exalt his | name together.

4   I sought the Lord | and he answered me
    and delivered me from | all my fears.

5   Look upon him and | be radiant
    and your faces shall not | be ashamed.

6   This poor soul cried, and the Lord heard me and saved me from | all my troubles.

7   The angel of the Lord encamps around those who fear him | and delivers them.

9   Fear the Lord, all you his | holy ones,
    for those who fear him | läck nothing.

10   Lions may lack and | suffer hunger,
    but those who seek the Lord lack nothing | that is good.

Proper 27
Continuous

Ps 78 v.1-7

R v.1b

PT

In - cline your ears to the words of my mouth.

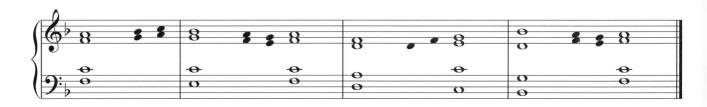

Incline your ears to the words of my mouth.

1   Hear my teaching O my people * incline your ears to the words of | my mouth.
2   I will open my mouth in a parable * I will pour forth mysteries | from of old,
3   Such as we have | heard and known,
     which our | <u>forebears</u> have told us.

4   We will not hide from their children but will recount to generations | to come,
     the praises of the Lord and his power and the wonderful works | he has done.
5   He laid a solemn charge on Jacob and made it a | law in Israel,
     which he commanded them to | teach their children,

6   That the generations to come might know and the children yet | unborn,
     that they in turn might tell it | to their children;
7   So that they might put their | trust in God
     and not forget the deeds of God but keep | his commandments,

Proper 27
Paired

R v.1   PT

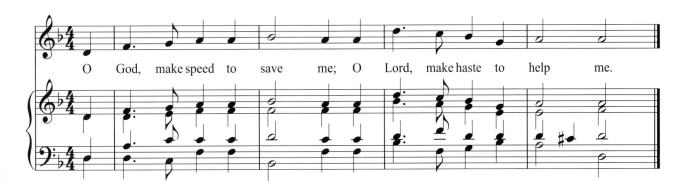

O God, make speed to save me; O Lord, make haste to help me.

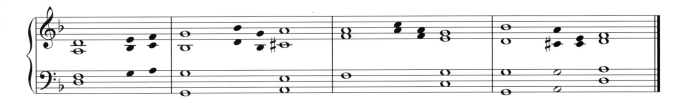

O God, make speed to save me;
O Lord, make haste to help me.

1   O God make speed | to save me;
     O Lord make | haste to help me.
2   Let those who seek my life be put to shame | and confusion;
     let them be turned back and disgraced who | wish me evil.

3   Let those who mock and | deride me
     turn back be|cause of their shame.
4   But let all who seek you rejoice | and be glad in you;
     let those who love your salvation say always | 'Great is the Lord!'

5   As for me I am poor | and needy;
     come to me | quickly O God.
6   You are my help and | my deliverer;
     O Lord do | not delay.

Proper 28
Continuous

Ps 123

R v.1

AJC

To you I lift up my eyes, to you that are enthroned in the heavens.

2 As the eyes of servants look to the hand of their <u>master</u>,
   or the eyes of a maid to the hand of her <u>mistress</u>,
3 So our eyes wait upon the Lord our <u>God</u>,
   until he have mercy up<u>on us</u>.

4 Have mercy upon us, O Lord, have mercy u<u>pon us</u>,
   for we have had more than enough of con<u>tempt.</u>
5 Our soul has had more than enough of the scorn of the <u>arrogant</u>,
   and of the contempt of the <u>proud</u>.

Proper 28
Paired

Lord, you have been our ref - uge from one gen-er-a-tion to a-no-ther.

Lord, you have been our refuge from one generation to another.

2   Before the mountains were brought forth or the earth and the world | were formed,
     from everlasting to everlasting | you are God.
3   You turn us back to | dust and say:
     'Turn back O | children of earth.'

4   For a thousand years in your sight are but | as yesterday,
     which passes like a | watch in the night.
5   You sweep them a|way like a dream;
     they fade away suddenly | like the grass.

6   In the morning it is green | and flourishes;
     in the evening it is | dried up and withered.
7   For we consume away in | your displeasure;
     we are afraid at your wrathful | indignation.

8   You have set our misdeeds | before you
     and our secret sins in the | light of your countenance.
12   So teach us to | number our days
     that we may apply our | hearts to wisdom.

Proper 29
Continuous

Ps 100
R v.1

AJC

O be joyful in the Lord, all the earth.

1b Serve the Lord with <u>glad</u>ness
    and come before his presence with a <u>song</u>.
2 Know that the Lord is <u>God</u>;
   it is he that has made us and we are his; we are his people and the sheep of his <u>pasture</u>.

3 Enter his gates with thanksgiving and his courts with <u>praise</u>;
   give thanks to him and bless his <u>name</u>.
4 For the Lord is gracious; his steadfast love is ever<u>lasting</u>,
   and his faithfulness endures from generation to gen<u>era</u>tion.

Proper 29

Paired

PT

For the Lord is a great God and a great king a-bove all gods.

For the Lord is a great God and a great king above all gods.

1   O come let us sing to | the Lord;
        let us heartily rejoice in the rock of | our salvation.
2   Let us come into his | <u>presence</u> with thanksgiving
        and be glad in | him with psalms.

4   In his hand are the depths of | the earth
        and the heights of the mountains | are his also.
5   The sea is his | for he made it,
        and his hands have | <u>moulded</u> the dry land.

6   Come let us worship and | bow down
        and kneel before the | Lord our Maker.
7   For he | is our God;
        we are the people of his pasture and the | <u>sheep of</u> his hand.

8   O that today you would listen to | his voice:
        'Harden not your hearts as at Meribah * on that day at Massah | in the wilderness,
9   'When your forebears tested me and put me | to the proof,
        though they had | seen my works.

10   'Forty years long I detested that generation | and said,
        "This people are wayward in their hearts * they do not | know my ways."
11   'So I swore | in my wrath,
        "They shall not enter | <u>into</u> my rest." '

APPENDIX 1

Festivals

Festival	Date	Psalm	Page
The Naming and Circumcision of Jesus	1 January	8	27
The Conversion of St Paul	25 January	67	52
St Brigid	1 February	134	81
St Patrick	17 March	145.1-13	82
St Joseph of Nazareth	19 March	89.26-36	83
The Annunciation of Our Lord to the BVM	25 March	40.5-10	84
St Mark	25 April	119.9-16	Yr B 32
St Philip and St James	1 May	119.1-8	10
St Matthias	14 May	15	8
The Visitation of the Blessed Virgin Mary	31 May	113	Yr C 81
St Columba	9 June	34.9-15	85
St Barnabas	11 June	112.1-9	9
The Birth of St John the Baptist	24 June	85.7-13	86
St Peter	29 June	125	Yr B 71
St Thomas	3 July	31.1-6	87
St Mary Magdalene	22 July	42.1-10	88
St James	25 July	126	Yr B 3, Yr C 32
The Transfiguration of Our Lord	6 August	97	Yr B 7, Yr C 52
St Bartholomew	24 August	145.1-7	82
The Birth of the Blessed Virgin Mary	8 September	45.10-17	38
St Matthew	21 September	119.65-72	89
St Michael and All Angels	29 September	103.19-22	90
St Philip the Deacon	11 October	119.105-112	40
St Luke	18 October	147.1-7	91
St James, the Brother of Our Lord	23 October	1	70
St Simon and St Jude	28 October	119.89-96	92
St Andrew	30 November	19.1-6	65
St Stephen	26 December	119:161-168	93
St John	27 December	117	94
The Holy Innocents	28 December	124	53

St Brigid

Ps 134

R v.1a

AJC

Come, bless the Lord, ___ all ___ you ser - vants of the Lord.

1   Come, bless the <u>Lord</u>,
     all you servants of the <u>Lord</u>,
     you that by night <u>stand</u>
     in the house of the <u>Lord</u>.

2   Lift up your hands towards the <u>sanctuary</u>
     and bless the <u>Lord</u>.

3   The Lord who made heaven and <u>earth</u>
     give you blessing out of <u>Zion</u>.

St Patrick

Ps 145 v.1-13

R v.1   PT

I will exalt you, O God, my King, and bless your name for ever and ever.

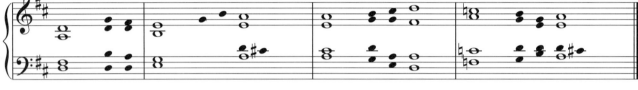

I will exalt you, O God my King,
and bless your name for ever and ever.

2   Every day will | I bless you
    and praise your name for | ever and ever.
3   Great is the Lord and highly | to be praised;
    his greatness is beyond all | searching out.

4   One generation shall praise your works | to another
    and declare your | mighty acts.
5   They shall speak of the majesty | of your glory,
    and I will tell of all your | wonderful deeds.

6   They shall speak of the might of your marvel|lous acts,
    and I will also | tell of your greatness.
7   They shall pour forth the story of your a|bundant kindness
    and joyfully | sing of your righteousness.

8   The Lord is gracious | and merciful,
    long-suffering | and of great goodness.
9   The Lord is | loving to everyone
    and his mercy is over | all his creatures.

10 All your works praise you | O Lord,   12   To make known to all peoples your migh|ty acts
    and your faithful | servants bless you.   and the glorious splendour | of your kingdom.
11 They tell of the glory | of your kingdom   13   Your kingdom is an ever|lasting kingdom;
    and speak of your | mighty power,   your dominion endures through|out all ages.

On St Bartholomew's Day v.8-13 are omitted

St Joseph of Nazareth

Ps 89
R v.52

AJC

Blessed be the Lord for evermore. Amen and Amen.

26   'He shall call to me, "You are my <u>Father</u>,
      my God, and the rock of my sal<u>vation</u>;"
27   'And I will make him my <u>firstborn</u>,
      the most high above the kings of the <u>earth</u>.

28   'The love I have pledged to him will I keep for <u>ever</u>,
      and my covenant will stand <u>fast with him</u>.
29   'His seed also will I make to endure for <u>ever</u>
      and his throne as the days of <u>heaven</u>.

30   'But if his children forsake my <u>law</u>
      and cease to walk in my <u>judgements</u>,
31   'If they break my statutes and do not keep my com<u>mandments</u>,
32   'I will punish their offences with a rod and their sin with <u>scourges</u>.

33   'But I will not take from him my steadfast <u>love</u>
      nor suffer my truth to <u>fail</u>.
34   'My covenant will I not <u>break</u>
      nor alter what has gone out of my <u>lips</u>.

35   'Once for all have I sworn by my <u>holiness</u>
      that I will not prove false to <u>David</u>.
36   'His seed shall endure for <u>ever</u>
      and his throne as the sun before <u>me</u>.

The Annunciation of Our Lord
to the Blessed Virgin Mary

Ps 40 v.5-10

R v.4

PT

Bless-ed is the one who trusts in the Lord, who does not turn to the proud that fol - low a lie.

Blessed is the one who trusts in the Lord,
who does not turn to the proud that follow a lie.

5   Great are the wonders you have done O Lord my God * how great your | designs for us!
    There is none that can | be compared with you.

6   If I were to pro|claim them and tell of them
    they would be more than I am able | to express.

7   Sacrifice and offering you do not | desire
    but my ears | you have opened;

8   Burnt offering and sacrifice for sin you | have not required;
    then said I * | 'Lo I come.

9   'In the scroll of the book it is written of me that I should do your will O | my God;
    I delight to do it * your law is with|in my heart.'

10 I have declared your righteousness in the | great <u>congregation</u>;
    behold I did not restrain my lips, and that O | Lord you know.

St Columba

Ps 34 v 9-15

R v.3

AJC

Mag - ni - fy the Lord with me; let us ex - alt his name to - geth - er.

Magnify the Lord with me; let us exalt his name together.

9   Fear the Lord, all you his <u>holy ones</u>,
         for those who fear him lack <u>nothing</u>.

10   Lions may lack and suffer <u>hunger</u>,
         but those who seek the Lord lack nothing that is <u>good</u>.

11   Come, my children, and listen to <u>me</u>;
         I will teach you the fear of the <u>Lord</u>.

12   Who is there who delights in <u>life</u>
         and longs for days to enjoy <u>good things</u>?

13   Keep your tongue from evil and your lips from lying <u>words</u>.

14   Turn from evil and do good; seek peace and pur<u>sue it</u>.

15   The eyes of the Lord are upon the <u>righteous</u>
         and his ears are open to their <u>cry</u>.

The Birth of St John the Baptist

Ps. 85 v. 7-13

R. v. 7

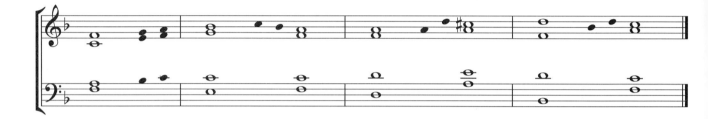

Show us your mercy, O Lord, and grant us your salvation.

8 I will listen to what the Lord God | will say,
   for he shall speak peace to his people and to the faithful, that they turn not a|gain to folly.

9 Truly, his salvation is near to | those who fear him,
   that his glory may dwell | in our land.

10 Mercy and truth are met | together,
   righteousness and peace have | kissed each other;

11 Truth shall spring up | from the earth
   and righteousness look | down from heaven.

12 The Lord will indeed give all that | is good,
   and our land will | yield its increase.

13 Righteousness shall | go before him
   and direct his steps | in the way.

St Thomas

Ps 31 v 1-6

R v.16

AJC

Make your face to shine upon your servant, an dsave me for your mercy's sake.

1   In you, O Lord, have I taken refuge; let me never be put to <u>shame</u>;
    deliver me in your <u>righteousness</u>.
2   Incline your <u>ear to me</u>;
    make haste to de<u>liver me</u>.

3   Be my strong rock, a fortress to save me, for you are my rock and my <u>stronghold</u>;
    guide me, and lead me for your <u>name's sake</u>.
4   Take me out of the net that they have laid secretly <u>for me</u>,
    for you are my <u>strength</u>.

5   Into your hands I commend my <u>spirit</u>,
    for you have redeemed me, O Lord God of <u>truth</u>.
6   I hate those who cling to worthless <u>idols</u>;
    I put my trust in the <u>Lord</u>.

St Mary Magdalene

O put your trust in God, for I will yet give him thanks, who is the help of my countenance and my God

1   As the deer longs for the water brooks * so longs my soul for you | O God.

2   My soul is athirst for God, even for the living God *
         when shall I come before the | <u>presence</u> of God?

3   My tears have been my bread | day and night,
    while all day long they say to me 'Where is | now your God?'

4   Now when I think on these things I pour out | my soul:
    how I went with the multitude and led the procession to the | house of God,

5   With the voice of | praise and thanksgiving
    among those who kept | holy day.

6   Why are you so full of heaviness O | my soul
    and why are you so dis|<u>quieted</u> within me?

8   My soul is | <u>heavy</u> within me;
    therefore I will remember you from the land of Jordan *
         and from Hermon and the | hill of Mizar.

9   Deep calls to deep in the thunder of | your waterfalls;
    all your breakers and | <u>waves have</u> gone over me.

10   The Lord will grant his loving-kindness | in the daytime;
    through the night his song will be with me, a prayer to the | <u>God of</u> my life.

St Matthew

Ps 119 v.65-72
R v.68b

PT

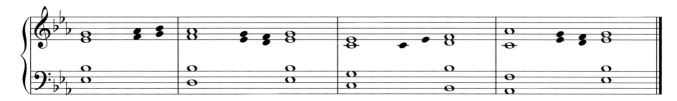

O Lord, teach me your statutes.

65   You have dealt graciously with | your servant,
        according to your | word O Lord.
66   O teach me true under|standing and knowledge,
        for I have trusted in | your commandments.

67   Before I was afflicted I went | astray,
        but now I | keep your word.
68   You are gracious | and do good;
        O Lord | teach me your statutes.

69   The proud have smeared me | with lies,
        but I will keep your commandments with my | whöle heart.
70   Their heart has become | gross with fat,
        but my delight is | in your law.

71   It is good for me that I have been | afflicted,
        that I may | learn your statutes.
72   The law of your mouth is | dearer to me
        than a hoard of | gold and silver.

St Michael and All Angels

Ps 103 v.19-22
R Ps 91 v.11

PT

For he shall give his angels charge over you,
to keep you in all your ways.

19   The Lord has established his throne | in heaven,
        and his kingdom has dominion | over | all.

20   Bless the Lord you | <u>angels</u> of his,
        you mighty ones who do his bidding * and hearken to the voice | of his word.

21   Bless the Lord all you | his hosts,
        you ministers of his who | do his will.

22   Bless the Lord all you works of his * in all places of | his dominion;
        bless the Lord | O my soul.

St Luke

Ps 147 v.1-7

R v.7

PT

Sing to the Lord with thanks-giv-ing;____ make mus-ic to our God up-on the lyre.

Sing to the Lord with thanksgiving;
make music to our God upon the lyre;

1   Alleluia * how good it is to make music for | our God,
    how joyful to honour | him with praise.
2   The Lord | builds up Jerusalem
    and gathers together the | outcasts of Israel.

3   He heals the bro|kenhearted
    and binds up | all their wounds.
4   He counts the | number of the stars
    and calls them | all by their names.

5   Great is our Lord and mighty | in power;
    his wisdom is be|yond all telling.
6   The Lord | lifts up the poor,
    but casts down the wicked | to the ground.

St Simon and St Jude

Ps 119 v.89-96
R v.89

AJC

O Lord, your word is everlasting; it ever stands firm in the heavens.

89 O Lord, your word is ever<u>last</u>ing;
    it ever stands firm in the <u>heav</u>ens.

90 Your faithfulness also remains from one generation to an<u>other</u>;
    you have established the earth and it a<u>bides</u>.

91 So also your judgements stand firm this <u>day</u>,
    for all things are your <u>servants</u>.

92 If your law had not been my de<u>light</u>,
    I should have perished in my <u>trouble</u>.

93 I will never forget your com<u>mandments</u>,
    for by them you have given me <u>life</u>.

94 I am yours, O <u>save me</u>!
    For I have sought your com<u>mandments</u>.

95 The wicked have waited for me to des<u>troy me</u>,
    but I will meditate on your <u>testimonies</u>.

96 I have seen an end of all per<u>fection</u>,
    but your commandment knows no <u>bounds</u>.

St Stephen

Ps 119 v.161-168

R v.164

AJC

Sev-en times a day do I praise you, be-cause of your right-eous judg - ments.

Seven times a day do I praise you, because of your righteous judgements.

161   Princes have persecuted me without a <u>cause</u>,
        but my heart stands in awe of your <u>word</u>.

162   I am as glad of your <u>word</u>
        as one who finds great <u>spoils</u>.

163   As for lies, I hate and ab<u>hor them</u>,
        but your law do I <u>love</u>.

164   Seven times a day do I <u>praise you</u>,
        because of your righteous <u>judgements</u>.

165   Great peace have they who love your <u>law</u>;
        nothing shall make them <u>stumble</u>.

166   Lord, I have looked for your sal<u>vation</u>
        and I have fulfilled your com<u>mandments</u>.

167   My soul has kept your <u>testimonies</u>
        and greatly have I <u>loved them</u>.

168   I have kept your commandments and <u>testimonies</u>,
        for all my ways are be<u>fore you</u>.

St John

Ps 117
R Alleluia

AJC

Alleluia.

1 O praise the Lord, all you <u>nations</u>;
  praise him, all you <u>peoples</u>.

2 For great is his steadfast love to<u>wards us</u>,
  and the faithfulness of the Lord endures for <u>ever</u>.

APPENDIX 2

The Easter Vigil

Psalm after Genesis 1:1-2-4a

Ps 136 v.1-9, 23-26

R v.1a

for his mer - cy en - dures for ev - er.

1   Give thanks to the Lord for he | is gracious,
for his mercy endures for ever.

2   Give thanks to the God | of gods,
for his mercy endures for ever.

3   Give thanks to the Lord | of lords,
for his mercy endures for ever;

4   Who alone does | great wonders,
for his mercy endures for ever;

5   Who by wisdom made | the heavens,
for his mercy endures for ever;

6   Who laid out the earth upon | the waters,
for his mercy endures for ever;

7   Who made the | great lights,
for his mercy endures for ever;

8   The sun to rule | the day,
for his mercy endures for ever;

9   The moon and the stars to govern | the night,
for his mercy endures for ever;

23   Who remembered us when we were | in trouble,
for his mercy endures for ever;

24   And delivered us from | our enemies,
for his mercy endures for ever;

25   Who gives food to | all creatures,
for his mercy endures for ever.

26   Give thanks to the God | of heaven,
for his mercy endures for ever.

Canticle after Exodus 14

Exodus 15 v.1b-13, 17-18

R v.18

The Lord will reign for ev - ver and ev - er.

The Lord will reign for ever and ever.'

1 'I will sing to the Lord for he has tri|umphed gloriously;
   horse and rider he has thrown | into the sea.
2 The Lord is my strength and my might, and he has become | my salvation;
   this is my God, and I will praise him, my father's God, and | I will exalt him.

3 The Lord is | a warrior;
   the Lord | is his name.
4 'Pharaoh's chariots and his army he cast | into the sea;
   his picked officers were sunk | in the Red Sea.

5 The | floods covered them;
   they went down into the depths | like a stone.
6 Your right hand, O Lord | glorious in power—
   your right hand, O Lord | shattered the enemy.

7 In the greatness of your majesty you overthrew | your adversaries;
   you sent out your fury, it con|sumed them like stubble.
8 At the blast of your nostrils the waters piled up, the floods stood | up in a heap;
   the deeps congealed in the | heart of the sea.

9 The enemy said, "I will pursue, I will overtake,
      I will divide the spoil, my desire shall have | its fill of them.
   I will draw my sword, my | hand shall destroy them."
10 You blew with your wind, the sea | covered them;
   they sank like lead in the | mighty waters.

11 'Who is like you, O Lord, among | the gods?
   Who is like you, majestic in holiness,
      awesome in splendour, | doing wonders?
12 You stretched out | your right hand,
   the earth | swallowed them.

13 'In your steadfast love you led the people
      whom you | redeemed;
   you guided them by your strength
      to your | holy abode.
17 You brought them in and planted them on the
      mountain of your | own possession,
   the place, O Lord, that you made your abode,
      the sanctuary, O Lord, that your
         hands | have established.

Psalm after Ezekiel 37:1-14

Ps 143

R v.2a

PT

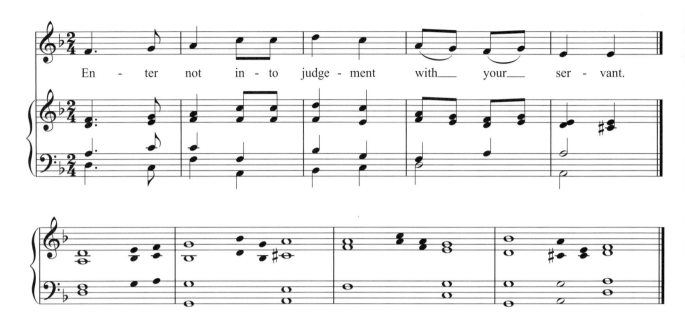

Enter not into judgement with your servant.

1   Hear my prayer, O Lord, and in your faithfulness give ear to my supp|lications;
       answer me | in your righteousness.

2   Enter not into judgement | with your servant,
       for in your sight shall no one | <u>living</u> be justified.

3   For the enemy has pursued me, crushing my life | <u>to the</u> ground,
       making me sit in darkness like | those long dead.

4   My spirit | faints within me;
       my heart with|<u>in me</u> is desolate.

5   I remember the time past; I muse upon all | your deeds;
       I consider the | works <u>of your</u> hands.

6   I stretch | out my hands to you;
       my soul gasps for you like a | thirsty land.

7   O Lord, make haste to answer me; my spi|rit fails me;
       hide not your face from me lest I be like those who go | down <u>to the</u> Pit.

8   Let me hear of your loving-kindness in the morning, for in you I | put my trust;
       show me the way I should walk in, for I lift | up my soul to you.

9   Deliver me, O Lord, from | my enemies,
       for I flee to | you for refuge.

10   Teach me to do what pleases you, for | <u>you are</u> my God;
       let your kindly spirit lead me on a | level path.

11   Revive me, O Lord, for | your name's sake;
       for your righteousness' sake, bring me | out of trouble.

12   In your faithfulness, slay my enemies, and destroy all the adversaries | of my soul,
       for truly | <u>I am</u> your servant.

Index of Psalms – Year A

Index of Responses – Year A

Master Index to Years A, B and C